# Praises For:

# Addicted to Hope

Michelle had the kind of life that most people would have walked away from and never looked back. But even when she was broke, practically homeless, and suddenly a single-parent of three boys, Michelle hoped against all hope. This passion and hope is in the fiber of Michelle's being still today. As Pastors, we have watched Michelle stand and pray for her family, stand for the rights of unborn children, stand in faith through her own physical battles and each time we see hope arise even stronger. Michelle's not ashamed or embarrassed of her past life, but instead, she recognizes her story as a tool that can give others hope to know, that they too can overcome.

**—Pastor Charlie & Tamera Muller**

So glad to see this book come to print. As a Pastor with Victory Christian Church, heading up the jail ministry. I have known Michelle and John for 10 years. This book will touch many lives. I witnessed this 1st hand, when Michelle told her side of their story of raising her children while her husband was incarcerated. There wasn't a dry eye in the house, at Albany County Jail, including mine.

**—Pastor Marty Stanton**

I am elated to finally see this book come to fruition. I have known both Michelle and her husband for 10 years and have always been in awe of this truly amazing story of both restoration and redemption through the power of Jesus Christ. I know this book will be an incredible source of encouragement to so many and that God is still in the miracle business even today. All the Glory to God.

**— Darlene Stanton**, *Pastor Marty Stanton's wife*

We are thrilled to finally see Michelle's powerful testimony in print. It has been a blessing and a privilege to walk beside Michelle and her husband John as their Pastors ever since Michelle, with three little boys and a broken heart, moved into our neighborhood all those years ago. Since then, we've been witnesses over and over again to the active and mighty Hand of God at work in their lives. Miracles, healings, supernatural financial provision, and so much more are all a part of this amazing journey! As you walk with Michelle through her story, we pray that her determination and unquenchable faith in Jesus Christ will reach out to you from these pages to build your spirit and remind you that God is with you and FOR you. Through this book, may you be encouraged to keep moving forward with God, no matter the circumstances, and to believe that what God has so faithfully done in Michelle and John's lives, He can do for you, too.

**—Pastor Charles and Joyce Gay**

I have known Michelle Mulledy for almost 15 years. Her true story of faith through hardship, heartbreak and eventually joyous breakthrough will encourage so many hearts around the globe. Michelle and her husband John have experienced God's tenacious love, mercy and redemption in every area of life. Her moving and compelling testimony will surely help others stand strong during life's very difficult challenges. I'm so glad to call both Michelle and John my good friends! I know this book will tremendously bless all those that read it."

**Liz Joy,** *Candidate for United States Congress NY 20th District*

Discover how one married couple pried loose the deadly grip of drug addiction successfully. A strong wife (Michelle Mulledy) coping with an opioid-addicted husband (John Mulledy), in this true story brought together by authors Nancy Duci Denofio and Jo Anne Mitchum, readers get to go on the amazing journey of a prayerful wife.

**—Barbara Garro**, M.A. host of *5 Minutes with Jesus Alive Radio Network Show.*

# ADDICTED TO HOPE

Jo Anne Mitchum & Nancy Duci Denofio

Published by KHARIS PUBLISHING, imprint of KHARIS MEDIA LLC.

Copyright © 2022 Jo Anne Mitchum and Nancy Duci Denofio

ISBN-13: 978-1-63746-119-8
ISBN-10: 1-63746-119-4

Library of Congress Control Number: 2022934500

All Scripture quotations, unless otherwise indicated, are taken from The Holy Bible, New International Version ®, NIV®. Copyright ©1973, 1978, 1984, 2011 by Biblical, Inc.™ Used by permission. All rights reserved worldwide.

All KHARIS PUBLISHING products are available at special quantity discounts for bulk purchase for sales promotions, premiums, fund-raising, and educational needs. For details, contact:

Kharis Media LLC
Tel: 1-479-599-8657
support@kharispublishing.com
www.kharispublishing.com

*This book is dedicated to our loving husbands who generously offer their enduring support.*

# Table of Contents

# 01
## Chapter

*Circle of Addiction*
*1967*

John dresses early for school. His third-grade uniform is the same as every other day, but John knows today is going to be different. He has a plan and today is the day he will execute. Leaning in with his ear flat against the bedroom door, he listens for his mother's footsteps. This is the moment he's waited for. He can feel it. His world is about to change.

After waiting all summer, September has finally arrived and with that, school is starting. John's gaze shifts toward the open window facing the front yard, where he can see the towering maple tree and hear voices carried in on the cool morning breeze. Outside, the street is already moving and bustling.

Soon the leaves will be changing on that big maple tree out front. Inside, things never seem to change. Winter, spring, summer or fall. Always the same. He knows he must make his own plans if he wants to see something change. John may only be eight, but he's old enough to know that change can be a good thing. He not only knows what must change in this house, but he also has a pretty good idea of how to make it happen. John has a plan.

Ignorant of that plan, John's father was startled to see him enter the kitchen earlier than usual for a bowl of cereal and cup of milk. Following a regular routine himself, his father had rolled out of bed, mumbled a few unrecognizable words of goodbye to John's mother, and then just as John encountered him, he was opening the back door about to head off to work. John didn't think he'd set his father too far behind schedule by coming downstairs earlier than usual.

It was still early before the sun lit the sky, and his father was on his way to the bridge that led him into Boston. His father worked at Boston City Hospital. That's where he'd met John's mother. She was only twenty-eight when they married; his father fifty-one at the time. This is his father's second marriage. John's father works as a Steward in charge of purchasing supplies for the hospital. His mother is interested in supplies too, but for a different reason.

Known as Eugene and Eleanor to their neighbors, the newlyweds moved into their current home on Summit Avenue in Brookline, Massachusetts. John's older brother, Eugene, Jr., was born first and after that, John came along and joined them in their first-floor apartment.

John walked through the cozy little apartment headed back to his bedroom, where he then listened to his mother lumber around the kitchen. He heard the odd spoon clanking in the sink, his mother's slippered feet scuffing over the faded linoleum, and her melodic voice as she talked to the television. A lot of mornings he'd hear her singing, especially when she was in a good mood. His mother was a very pretty lady, much younger than his father. He sometimes wondered why she married an old man.

"Don't call for me. Keep it normal," John's mind silently ordered. He listened for the sound of her feet bringing her closer. Soon, he would hear the old creak of the handle twisting on the bathroom door, followed by the sound of the metal innards of the lock clicking into place. Listening, his legs rocked back and forth, feet shifting side to side. John knew if any small thing changed in the morning routine, he would have to postpone everything. All his planning and all his patience would be for naught.

Then he heard it. The lock clicked home and John slowly exhaled his relief. His mom would be setting her ash tray on the white porcelain tub and soon after she'd be lighting up a cigarette for her morning smoke. He was counting on her becoming engrossed with the morning paper. The time was upon him! This is what he'd been waiting for!

Normally, John would spend more time at home with his mother in the morning before walking by himself to school. He kind of liked it that way. At the very least, he'd gotten used to it. Eugene left early and, besides that, he'd let it be known that having a tag-a-long little brother wasn't cool. Typically, John would dilly dally until the very last second and then head off to school. He didn't have to worry about being late because the nuns at his school loved him. On this particular morning, however, thoughts of St. Gabriel's School were far from his mind.

Last night he'd stared at the shiny black hands against the white face of his alarm clock for a long time. They barely seemed to move. He was anxious for those two gold bells on top to ring him awake in the morning. Before he finally dozed off to sleep, he prayed out loud to God, not something he usually did. Getting down on his knees, he asked for an important favor, "God, if you ever do anything for me, please don't let me get caught in the morning." After he prayed, he made the sign of the cross, looked up at the ceiling and hoped that God was listening.

John was afraid he'd be beaten half to death when he returned from school in the afternoon, but that would be okay; he was accustomed to a good swat now and then. He looked to heaven again before getting up from his knees, "I want to see my mother change."

This morning, quiet as a church mouse, John tiptoed out from behind the old wooden door and made his way quickly down the flight of stairs. Based on how things were progressing, he believed that God had listened to his prayers last night. Skipping the third cellar step because it always creaks, he pictured his mother in the pink housecoat that his dad had given the boys money to buy last Christmas.

Not bothering to turn on the light, he made his way straight to the far-right corner. He flipped back an itchy wool blanket from a large pile of boxes. Even though nothing appeared outwardly dangerous, John knew better. Beneath that blanket was his mother's stash.

Starting with a bottle of Seagram's Seven, John held onto the bottle with shaking hands and began to pour the contents down a storm drain.

## Addicted To Hope

The smell of fresh whiskey punched him in the nose. He grabbed a second bottle, still wrapped in tissue paper. Unscrewing each top, he continued pouring the contents down the drain, one bottle at a time, one after another. The drain seemed to talk to him, gurgles of liquor swirling in circles. A few of the bottles were harder than the others to open, but John was determined not to leave a single ounce of liquor behind for his mother to drink.

A few bottles were wrapped in Christmas paper with tags dangling from them. "Geez, how many does she have," his young mind wondered. He also pondered why people would give her a gift like liquor instead of something she could use, like new slippers to go with her pretty pink robe? He quickened the pace, knowing there wasn't much time left to empty the remainder. Rushing as fast as an eight-year-old could, he replaced the empty bottles back in the boxes and covered them with the old blanket. John had to make it out of the house before his mother came back to the kitchen for another cup of coffee.

As much as John loved his mother, his heart broke, and he couldn't help but resent her on days of broken promises. He encountered a day like that last Thursday when she dragged him home by the shoulder, carrying another bottle of liquor. He'd just wanted a simple ice cream cone, one that she'd already promised him. Instead, she suddenly turned on him and treated him like he'd done something wrong. At the same time, she smiled at anybody who passed them by on the street.

He looked back at the blanket that had covered the coveted stash for a second longer and then mumbled out loud to himself, "She will never have a drink again. She will never have a drink again and I will be in big trouble tonight after school."

It was time. He ran upstairs, made a quick right through the back door and stumbled onto the back porch. He leaped over the wooden rail and ran as fast as his feet would carry him through high weeds taller than his growing eight-year-old frame. His small legs flew across the field and his eyes focused on the tall buildings in the distance where St. John of God Hospital stared menacingly back at him.

When he reached the end of the field, he sat down, leaned his head against a stone wall and gazed toward the bright blue sky. Last night he talked to God and now he was going to thank God for listening.

He reached into the pocket of his unpressed shirt and pulled out a bent cigarette he had taken from his mother's pack. He struck a match and lit his crooked cig, holding the smoke in his lungs until he couldn't hold his breath any longer. This kind of thing would make most kids in the third grade ill, but not John. He'd been swiping cigarettes from his mother's pack for at least a year. His thoughts went back to the kind of reception he'd receive when he got back home. "I can take it," he told himself, "And she won't have her drink anymore."

John knew his grandmother would be there if he needed her. Sometimes after school he would head upstairs instead of to his apartment on the first floor. His mother never cared if he stopped for a visit, and this would be a perfect day to spend with his grandmother. He'd stay there until his father came home from work.

He lit a second cigarette and continued to talk to himself, "I'm already in trouble. So, what the heck, another cigarette won't kill me... but my mother might." After he took his final drag, he smashed the cigarette into the dirt with the toe of his shoe. Sister Superior would frown at the dirt on his shoes, but that was the least of his worries today.

Soon after that memorable day, both of John's parents became members of Alcoholics Anonymous (AA). Eugene and Eleanor walked away from drinking and AA became a big part of all their lives. Eugene had hoped that the damage caused in the boys' early life could in some way be reversed by attending the nightly AA meetings. Unfortunately, the damage wasn't that easily undone.

Looking back, I understood that John and his brother Gene were used to a lot of turmoil and upheaval in their lives. Gene, who was two years older, was more of a tough guy and always getting into fights with other kids. John was more even tempered. At school, John saw Gene getting bullied and did his best to step in and make it stop. At home, their roles reversed, and Gene took more abuse from their parents in an attempt to protect John. They leaned on one another since in their younger days when they didn't receive much support from their parents.

The first seven years of John's life were unstable with John and his brother sometimes being removed from their home and placed into foster care. Eugene and Eleanor were unable to care for the boys because they were in and out of facilities to dry out from incessant alcohol abuse. Thankfully, the stays at foster homes were always temporary, but when the boys were separated, it made the stays seem even longer.

Once when it was just their mom in a facility and their father couldn't care for the boys due to his having to work, they stayed at a place called Nazareth's: A Home for Little Wanderers. Their dad would visit the boys on Saturday's, but no matter how much they'd beg, Eugene wouldn't bring them home. It must have broken his heart, but at the same time, those little boys couldn't understand and surely felt abandoned.

While not every experience in John's young life was bad, there were more than enough troubles that his adult life was negatively impacted.

# 02
## Chapter

*Tipping Point*
*1989*

A quick look in the rearview mirror and I could see little John give Ryan a shove. "Knock it off, boys. We've got a busy night ahead of us. We don't have a whole lot of time. While you guys are eating, I'll grab the costumes. We don't want to be late for your school Christmas play!"

Tapping the right directional, I headed toward the two-family house that we shared with my parents. A day just like every other, my time was filled caring for my three boys. Up ahead, the house lit up like a Christmas tree. It took me a minute to realize that the flashing lights weren't from all the holiday decorations… Red and blue lights flashing, police cars marked both sides of the street. Fear in my heart made me want to speed down the rest of the street while dread in my belly warned me to slow down.

"Boys, you stay in the car while I find out what's going on!" I barked as I pulled over in front of the house and ran to the nearest policeman.

Never had I seen so many police officers in one place. It couldn't be good.

"Officer, I'm Michelle Mulledy and I live on the first floor. My parents live above, but they're on vacation. Please tell me what's going on!" A quick look back to the car told me the boys had stayed put and I hand motioned that they remain there.

I could also see a woman standing outside the house next door. I recognized her as the woman living in the upstairs apartment and she looked pretty shook up. Several police officers were standing with her.

The feeling in the pit of my stomach was getting worse. There were at least a dozen police officers clustered on my front lawn and more next door. It was then that I spotted my husband, my estranged husband, John. Tangled in the midst of this chaotic scene, John was being led to one of the police cruisers restrained by handcuffs.

My mind couldn't process the surreal scene laid out before me. My husband's blank eyes never even noticed me breaking apart just a few yards away. How could they? I knew by the look he wore that he was high on his current drug of choice.

Turning back to check on the boys, I noticed one of the police officers had gathered them up and was escorting them into the house, away from the confusing drama unfolding on their front yard. Grateful for that, I turned back to the officer near me and this time demanded to know what was happening.

Standing there, overwhelmed by the sight of what had become of my husband, my heart was heavy with grief for the dream I had continued to cling to. My dream was no different than most women my age. I wasn't looking for white picket fences, but I was looking for a husband that came home every night; sober.

The past eighteen months we'd been living a nightmare. With John in and out of drug and alcohol rehabilitation centers, my sons and I were forced to move in with my parents. John was in no shape to manage his highly regarded automobile repair shop in Boston and without that income, we were struggling to pay our bills. Thank God for my parents and their offer to take us in.

There were stipulations though. After we figured out that John was sneaking in and stealing from us, wedding gifts in the basement hocked for drug money, my father insisted that the locks be changed. That's why I was so shocked when the officer told me that John had jumped from the upstairs bathroom window. How was that even possible?

It wasn't like John hadn't tried to get clean. He promised me that he would. Again and again. In the past year and a half, he'd been in and out of six different rehab centers. He never stayed long enough to complete even a single one of them. My father and I begged the court to remand him to a state run facility, but the court turned us down. They said he'd need to commit a crime before that would happen. Looking at John in the patrol car, I thought that maybe now John would get the help he desperately needed.

Life with John was a rollercoaster. I was always waiting for the shoe to drop. It was never a matter of if but of when. He'd clean up for a few days, sometimes even a few weeks at a time. Unfortunately, that never lasted. Despite all his well-intentioned promises, John always went back on his word.

After endless months of police being beckoned to the house, abandoned counselors, and broken promises, I asked John to leave. I couldn't bear to live that way anymore and I couldn't bear the impact that these dreadful ups and downs were having on our children.

John was living on the streets now. It pained me to think about that, but I couldn't make his choices for him. I'd tried that and it didn't work. Obviously, sometimes I'd see him standing around in Brighton Center when I'd be driving by. The boys would spot him now and again, pleading for me to stop and pick him up. How is it possible that I have any more heart left to break?

How do I explain to my sons, the oldest only 6 years old, that their father had to hit bottom before he could get better? Seriously, how does a mother do that? I certainly never wanted my boys to think I'd abandon them on the street if they were ever in need. Still, each time I kept driving.

To say I was a mess would be an understatement. I was just trying to survive from one day to the next. My priority was to give my boys shelter, put food in their bellies, and make sure they knew they were loved. That was my purpose in life. Anything beyond that, I didn't have the energy to entertain. I was really grateful for all the help that my parents gave me with the boys. They provided an example of stability that my own life was lacking. I couldn't do it without them.

**Addicted To Hope**

The police car pulled away with my broken husband slumped in the back seat. I wasn't sure what tomorrow would bring, but I knew what my next steps would be. I marched into the living room and rounded up the boys. "Let's grab some sandwiches, boys. We've got to hurry if we're going to make the Christmas Play tonight!"

# 03
## Chapter

## *Point of Departure*

That night, with another successful Christmas performance in the books, the boys and I headed over to my cousin Nancy's. As strong as I was, I didn't want to be alone in that house. My emotions were still reeling from what we'd seen transpire before I took the boys to their Christmas Play. The boys themselves were distracted and tired out from their school activities and fell off to sleep as soon as they went to bed.

When I climbed into bed that night, I screamed into a pillow already soaked from my tears. I kept thinking about the children. They were growing up without a father present. Not only that but our money was gone. If we didn't live in my parent's house, we'd be out on the street too.

No sleep came to me that night. Instead, I laid there and thought about how the love I'd once had for John was beginning to turn into hate. I was so tired of him turning our lives upside down. He was causing turmoil in the boys' lives too. When I remembered how John had described his own childhood, I became afraid of the impact all this would have on our children.

**Addicted To Hope**

As much as I appreciated all the support that my parents provided, I was really glad that they weren't home to see this latest event. Being away, they wouldn't have to read about their son-in-law in the paper. I don't know why, but that mattered to me. I stared at the ceiling and considered all the blood and glass I had to clean up before they got back. They had warned me not to let John in the house while they were gone. I kept my word, but John had broken in and made a mess anyway.

My parents told me time and again that I held false hope for our marriage. It was difficult to hear, but I understood why they said that. I couldn't imagine what it must have been like for them to watch their only daughter and grandsons living lives that were in constant upheaval. My situation must have been horrific for them to witness. Looking at things through their eyes, just for a moment, it came to me that maybe they were right. Maybe the situation really was hopeless. Maybe life was just too crazy with John in it.

That night was the beginning of the end to the craziness. It was a real turning point where I finally made the decision that I'd needed to make. I was finally ready for some serious changes. I'd had enough. This woman was done with the dream. I was letting go of the need for everything to work out perfectly in my marriage. As much as I wanted a normal life with my husband by my side, a husband who was healthy and happy while also being a loving and engaged father, I didn't have the strength to make it happen.

Rolling over, I thought about God. That was another relationship that I'd come close to giving up on. During one of his clean periods, John had welcomed Christ into his life and encouraged me to do the same. I balked at first. He gave me a Bible of my own with my name engraved on the cover. I looked at it and told him that he had the nerve to tell me about God when he was living the life that he'd been living. I screamed that he'd gone from drug addiction to being addicted to God. I didn't want any part of it then, but over time I'd started to forge my own relationship with Christ. I'd put that relationship on the back burner a few times but now seemed like the right time to resurrect that connection and lean on it. Lean on it in a way that I'd never done before. I decided right then and there that I needed to put my faith to work.

I felt strongly that it was time for me to step up, take action, and make sound choices. My boys needed stability. I needed stability. I needed to get out of the mess I found myself in and get on with life for my sake and the sake of the kids. I had a strong faith in God and all He could do in our lives, and I was open to His will for my family. I decided that night to place John's life in God's hands as well and remove myself and my kids from that situation. I also wanted to relieve my parents and my family of this constant turmoil. I was so afraid that my parents' health would be significantly impacted by the stress brought on by our struggle.

My feet touched the floor before the sun came up at my cousin's house. I tiptoed into Nancy's room, "Hey, I have to get over to the house this morning. Can you watch the boys a little longer? I need to get that window fixed before my parents get back home." My cousin and her husband Al, were a huge help to me. All of my cousins were. I was the oldest of all the grandchildren. My cousins Susan Marie, Susanna and her husband Mike were always there for me. I had a very close family and we helped each other. I will always be appreciative of my entire family who were also always there with strong support for my children.

Even though Nancy offered to help out at the house, I didn't want to bring the boys back until everything was cleaned up. Another neighbor was kind enough to help me with all that and by 8am, I had the house cleaned and the glass picked up. The window would be fixed that afternoon. I was a woman on a mission. By the time the boys got home from school, the house would look like nothing out of the ordinary had happened. I stopped back by Nancy's to check in with my youngest, but I couldn't take him with me yet. I had one more dreaded chore to do on my own. Leaving Daniel eating ice cream in the very capable hands of my cousin, I headed over to Brighton Police Station.

I wasn't sure if I was ready for this. In a way, I felt shut down. I was closed off from my former self. I no longer felt like John's wife. Not only was I feeling different, but the whole situation was different. In the past, I'd be going to visit John at a rehabilitation center. This time, I was going to see my husband at the police station. This time, he'd be doing jail time. This time, I no longer wanted to help him.

I opened the door to the courtroom and took a seat near the back. John was already there, sitting in a holding cell near the front of the courtroom. Before the proceedings started, his public defender came over to speak with me. He introduced himself to me, "Mrs. Mulledy, I knew John before this happened. As a matter of fact, I brought my car to him and he always did a great job. It's really sad what drugs have done to him. How are you coping with all of this?"

"It's hard, especially with the boys," I responded. Beside myself, I couldn't bring myself to look into the lawyer's eyes when he went on, "John is in a good deal of trouble. He could be looking at 20 years in prison." When I still didn't look up, he paused, "Did you hear me, Mrs. Mulledy?"

I was in shock. My entire body felt numb, limp. There was no peace to be found. My heart began to race, and my brain soon followed. I looked down at my hands where my thumbs twiddled out of control. Tears began to fill my eyes. All I could think about was John sitting like a caged animal for 20 years in a prison cell. I wondered what I might have done in my life to deserve this? We were in court to hear about John's punishment, but I felt like I was being punished for something too.

Memories kept flashing; our life broken down into snapshots. There were good times when John made me smile. He could make me feel like the most loved woman in the world. He knew exactly how to make me feel special. More times than not, however, all of John's energy went to finding his next fix. I reminded myself, that was how we ended up in court that cold day in December.

They were bringing John into the courtroom and I began to shake. Yet again, my heart was ripped in two. The man that I'd loved for more than half my life was standing before me in handcuffs. I avoided making eye contact with him.

The judge entered the courtroom and we were instructed to stand. After rifling through papers on his bench there was a decisive strike of his gavel and the judge stated, "Bail is set at $500,000." Just like that. Done. John was charged with Home Invasion, violating a restraining order, and drug possession. He was remanded back to jail.

I gasped. Tears flooded down my cheeks. In my shock and despair, I sat on that hard bench after the heavy bail was set and began to replay the last real conversation I had with John. It was the night I told him he had to leave. I remember the look on his face when he said, "I have nowhere to go." I told him then that I no longer had a place for him. I told him then that his reckless behavior would land him in jail or eventually kill him. Sitting in the courtroom, I realized that he was on his way to fulfilling that prophecy.

I couldn't bear to look at John. How many times did he beg to come back home, and I wouldn't let him? He begged me so often, telling me stories of sleeping on buses to keep warm at night and shivering in soaking wet clothes when the cold rains and then winter snow came. He said that he'd sit on the buses, nodding off or looking out the windows at the colored holiday lights they'd pass on the streets. He never knew what corner was next or where the driver would make him get off.

He said sometimes there were no buses as the snow piled up on the roads. When that was the case, he'd use his automotive skills to break into abandoned cars, making sure not to damage them, and he'd wait out the storms there. On the odd occasion he found a blanket in the car, he felt like he'd died and gone to heaven.

We were still in our own home when we had that last conversation, but it didn't completely end there. We'd talk from time to time, or rather, John would yell, and I would listen. He went from acting like a lost soul to an angry, bitter man. He started to berate me for living in a house that he paid for while he was sleeping on the streets. This wasn't accurate and he clearly wasn't in his right mind. He worried every night that he was going to be picked up by the cops and he blamed me for putting him at risk.

It was always hard to see him in that state. I'd sat there with my arms folded, trying to stay as still and quiet as possible. His emotional state was hanging on by a thread and I felt I didn't know my husband anymore. The John who was strung out was a stranger to me.

He then shared his fear that the drugs were making him hallucinate and he suspected the cops were looking for him. They'd heard that he was breaking into cars, which again was my fault in his eyes.

This man who just had bail set at half a million dollars had been a part of my life since I was just fifteen years old. On our wedding day, we vowed to love one another unconditionally. We committed to a relationship built on trust and to raising a family together. Had John really honored those vows though? I believed that I'd been the only one honoring them for years.

Looking at John sitting in the courtroom, I wondered exactly when we'd lost touch. For so long, I had no idea that he was struggling with his inner demons. I was blind to the darkness he was living in, the self-imposed prison of drugs and alcohol that he succumbed to. Apparently, the more money he'd made, the fancier the prison he'd built for himself, graduating from marijuana to drugs like cocaine and heroin. Now, he was finding himself in a real jail, heading toward a real prison.

As bad as I'd felt for him, I believed that it was his choice to live that way, not mine. I had to keep reminding myself of that, especially sitting in the cold and unforgiving courtroom.

I heard voices and brought my focus back to the courtroom where I saw John being led out of the courtroom. He had a limp. I imagined his fall from the upstairs window and lowered my eyes again.

An officer of the court approached me and told me that they were bringing John to the hospital to have him checked out from the fall. I glanced up at him and let him know without words that I was beyond caring.

Before he was out the door, I found the courage to walk over to John and whispered in his ear, "Stay away from me. Do not try to contact the kids or me. I hate you and never want to see you again." With that, I turned and walked out of the courtroom. I heard John screaming my name. I never looked back.

It was no surprise that John ignored my warning. Just one day later, he called me from Charles Street Jail in Boston. On the phone, I asked him what drove him to jump out the window. He told me a long story about what went through his mind during those days. He was definitely hallucinating and at that point was not even sure which house was the house that I grew up in. He wasn't exactly sure why he jumped, but he remembered being madder than a dog that he was relegated to being homeless.

From where he was sitting in jail, he could look back and see that he'd had a life, a family and that he knew real love. He was miserable thinking that his boys would grow up not knowing him. They'd change and do things that he wouldn't have the opportunity to experience with them. Instead, he was stuck behind bars rotting away by himself.

He realized now that he never lived for the future, but always for the day, the moment. He recalled that he'd never taken the time to visit the gravesites of his parents. It seemed like very scattered thinking when he hesitated for a moment and then confessed that he didn't know where all those thoughts were coming from. He was living between who he was, a respected businessman in his community, and what he'd become, a homeless person sitting in a jail cell. He clearly regretted losing what he had.

Even so, I felt incredibly disconnected from him then. I'd never understood what it felt like to be locked up behind bars without access to the outside world. I could not begin to know life so out of control that I was compelled to jump through glass, out of a second story window. I didn't want to understand. I didn't want to know what it was like to be controlled by a constant longing for drugs or to be caged in a cell.

What he went on to say cut me to the core. He shared with me that when he was doing drugs, it was just about the high. Intellectually I understood that was the addiction ruling his life. I knew that didn't shake his love for me or the kids, but it was still hard to hear that when he was using, he didn't think about me or the negative impact his actions had on our life together. After having three kids, it stung to know that our future was not in his thoughts.

John used our trip to the Bahamas to explain what he meant. I'd thought of that trip as our second honeymoon and a new beginning for us. Our original honeymoon was a red flag for me and I should have known back then that my life with John was going to be difficult, but I thought that getting married would change him. For some reason, I'd thought that our trip to the Bahamas would be different. It wasn't. Leading up to that trip, John hadn't been sleeping at night. One afternoon after work, he'd asked me to call the doctor and make an appointment for him. He was having anxiety attacks. He hoped the doctor could prescribe something to help with that. Of course, John never mentioned his issues with addiction to the doctor. When the doctor stopped prescribing Xanax to John, my husband turned to purchasing illegitimate scripts off the street. That stopped when his connection was arrested. The night before our trip John tried to obtain enough pain pills to get him through a week in the Caribbean, but that didn't work out.

Still frustrated and angry, the pills he'd taken before leaving for the airport were already starting to wear off and he was feeling pretty awful. He slept through most of the four-hour flight and once we landed, he headed straight for the beach. I headed to the front desk to check in but was informed that the room wouldn't be ready for another hour. I then headed down to join my husband on the beach and was stunned by the beautiful crystal blue water. There wasn't a cloud in the sky. It was paradise for a whole hour.

Sitting in the jail, John admitted on the phone that he'd bought a bag of dope on the beach. It was no surprise to me. I remembered when we got to our room; John had begun pacing back and forth. The Bohemian had sold my husband a beat bag, which I've since learned is a bad bag. At first, I was beyond angry at him. I envisioned the police arresting him and I made sure he understood the depth of my anger.

From there, things turned bad quickly. He collapsed onto the bed and began to roll back and forth, whining for drugs. He kept telling me there was something he had to tell me. I sat down next to him and his body started to shake. That was when he told me that he was using again. Not only was he using, but he'd started tripping with heroin and he felt like he was going to die without it.

I just sat there in shock. My brain couldn't process this new information. There I was in the beautiful Bahamas and my world was crashing around me. He was getting sicker by the minute. The more he told me what was going on, the more hysterical I got. I wanted to run out of the room and keep on going. I wanted to run from him and all of the pain he inflicted on me and our family.

Back then I had no idea what to expect as far as withdrawals from something like Heroin went. I sat there and cried for what felt like an eternity. I prayed for the first time in a very long time and cried out, "God I've heard about you all my life, but I don't know if you're real. If you are, I need your help." I cried myself to sleep, pleading with a God that I didn't really know to help John through the withdrawal because I knew it was more than I could handle alone.

When I woke up on the third day, still in the clothes I'd left home in, I prayed even harder for John. It wasn't long after that John also woke up and declared that he was feeling better than he'd expected. With things out in the open, John hoped we could salvage not only our trip but our marriage. He felt stronger and sure that he could kick drugs for good. I really just wanted to go home. I thought it was best to get back home before John itched for another bag. I had no doubt that day was coming.

On the way back to Boston, neither of us were talking as we were both dealing with what had transpired. On that call from jail John explained that, unbeknownst to me, when we were on the plane John was worrying about what might happen when we got back home. He shared that he'd peered out the window of the plane and looking into the clouds, he suddenly had a revelation that only God could help him break the chains of his addictions. It was believing that God would ensure that his life turned around that gave him the courage to embrace this epiphany and declare himself drug-free. For the first time in a long time, he'd felt alive again and he had hope. On the call John relayed that this was the start of his true relationship with God.

After talking about the Bahamas trip, John went on to tell me that he was really surprised the day that I informed him we were broke. That was when he was selling everything, including equipment from the garage, to buy heroin. Somehow, he thought I wouldn't find out what he was doing. That's not where his focus was. Rather, his mind was searching for his next high. He didn't think about when the money would run out. There were no consequences in John's world.

Back then, he thought that just telling me that he loved me should have been enough. But it wasn't. He could see that now. Still, he wondered how I could have been surprised by it all. We both knew that his parents were alcoholics. Substance abuse was in his genes. He even smoked grass in front of me when we were dating. Nobody seemed to mind back then. In fact, it seemed like everyone enjoyed his company back then, and I couldn't disagree with him, but things were different now. His addiction had gotten the better of him. I couldn't tolerate it any longer. I didn't tell John on the phone that day, but I was planning to take a trip.

The next day, I left Brighton with the boys in tow. My parents would be home in a few days and John's arrest would be in the pages of the local paper. I knew I couldn't face it and I didn't want the boys to have to live through that either. I made a call to my brother in Upstate New York and that's where we were headed. We were planning to stay with him for the weekend.

I couldn't stay in Brighton. Every time I looked out the window, I saw flashing lights and John being taken away in cuffs. It was hard to call my brother and tell him about the drama unfolding in my life, but it couldn't be avoided. I needed to get away.

I wasn't ready to face a repeat of the lying, begging, breaking out of rehab, and everything else that was on John's supposed path to recovery. I also wasn't ready to face my parents. I was sure that even though they wouldn't say it, they would be thinking "We told you so." Thankfully, my brother agreed with my approach to run away for a few days and tell them later.

The boys were actually excited to be going to visit their uncles in New York. Both of my brothers lived there in an area called Clifton Park and the boys had never been. As unsure as I was about this escape plan, when I packed the car and got the boys settled into the back seat, I began to feel my feet a little more solidly on the ground. I wondered if that was a little bit of my self-worth creeping back in. I barely recognized it.

I only grabbed a minimum amount of clothes to get us through the weekend. It was snowing and I was heading straight into a storm, but there was no turning back now. The drive was long because of the weather, but I had no time limits.

I didn't notice the beautiful snow capping the mountains of the Berkshires and I barely remember singing winter songs with the boys. My mind was spinning in circles. Thank God the boys decided to behave that day and only asked once to stop for a break on the highway. I really hadn't given money a thought. I knew I had enough gas to get to Clifton Park and that was all I cared about at that point. For maybe the first time, I was living in the moment too.

When the boys nodded off in the back seat, my thoughts turned to worry about providing for them. I asked God what I was supposed to do. I wanted to give my boys a better life. I didn't know how I'd do that without having any real job skills. I was petrified of what was going to happen to us.

I prayed silently as tears made a path down my cheeks. I was thankful that the boys were sleeping. I kept thinking of John even though I was determined to shut him out of my world. He'd kept calling me from the streets. Every time a stranger would lend him a quarter, he'd spent it on a call home to me. Hard as it was, I'd always listened to him.

I wasn't sure, whenever he'd make it back home for visits if he was coming home to see us or really there to steal something he could turn into drug money. I'd heard from a friend that he couldn't get his Percocet prescriptions anymore and was buying all of his drugs on the streets.

The weather on top of the mountain was the worst of the trip, but it let up once we got to the base and entered Lee, MA. I knew it wouldn't be long before we'd be reaching the New York state line and from there my brothers' place.

My thoughts drifted to my wonderful boys. John had been choking the life out of me, but he couldn't taint the joys of motherhood. My boys were my life now. I had to get them away from the pain their father wrought. We had to start over.

I pulled into the circular driveway where my brothers shared a townhouse. It was close to midnight and the house was still lit up. Joe met me at the door with warm hugs; Stephen was out of town at the time, traveling for work. The boys were still sleeping and my brother helped me carry them into the house. It gave us a chance to catch up in the kitchen.

I explained to him that I just couldn't face our parents and that on the long drive over I'd decided to look for a place to live in New York longer term. Joe wanted to know how I planned to accomplish this when I didn't have a penny to my name. While he agreed it was a good idea to move, he wasn't sure moving so far away from our parents would be wise right then. He also explained that the cost of living wasn't really different than back in Brighton.

I knew I'd figure it out. I'd gotten that far and I was confident that something good was about to happen. I knew that God would take care of me. I felt like a chick who'd been living inside an egg. The shell was suddenly cracking around me and I was about to experience the beauty of my world.

How was I so blessed to have found the Holy Spirit? How could I feel as strongly as I did that my life was saved after years of hell on earth? It was hard to make sense of, but I knew that my children depended on me, just like I was learning to depend on the Holy Spirit. They needed a chance to live a normal life and, with the grace of God, I was the one who had to give it to them.

When the newspaper arrived Sunday morning, I grabbed it and started looking for a home I could rent for the boys and me. I was also looking for a job that would give us enough to cover the rent.

Sipping his coffee across the table from me, Joe told me that I needed to be realistic. I stared directly into my brother's eyes and told him what I'd learned. I told him that God could do much more than anything we could ask or even imagine. Joe acquiesced and suggested I go ahead and circle the places I wanted to see. He even agreed to drive us to check them out.

Regardless of the incessant warnings to stay inside due to the blizzard conditions, I was moving forward with this and one house in particular jumped off the page at me. It was more expensive than I could afford, but I knew I'd be able to handle it. I just didn't know how.

In my mind, this was my one chance to change my life. It was time to start building a better life for my boys. If I didn't do this right now, I'd likely never make the changes that my boys and I needed. I knew that God was leading me in a different direction.

My brother looked at me and warned me not to be too brave. "You're still a woman in this world, alone with three children. Nothing is going to be easy." I was determined to prove him wrong.

The boys came into the kitchen washed, dressed, and all smiles. They loved their uncles and Joe had treated them to their favorite breakfast of pancakes. I was still focused on my search for a house to live in. There really weren't any houses on the page that I could afford, so I figured I might as well go after the one that was jumping out at me. I called and spoke to the owner, a woman who agreed to show me that house on Monday.

I'd told her that I didn't have a job at the moment but that I would have one before the rent was due. The look on my brother's face said he suspected that I wouldn't be able to afford it. I was confident that God was going to show me the way and referred often to Proverbs 3:5 "Trust in the Lord with all your heart and lean not on your own understanding. In all your ways acknowledge Him and He will direct your path."

Before I hung up, however, I asked the owner if she'd consider lowering the monthly rent by $100 and she agreed. We planned to see the house Monday morning at 10am, just before the boys and I headed back to Brighton. By the time my parents got home from vacation, I'd have a plan in place.

The rest of the day, Joe kept reminding me that I had no money. He kept asking how in the world I thought I could afford the chosen house or any house for that matter. I had no idea, but in my heart of hearts, I knew God would provide.

Later that night, I laid in bed and imagined a new house, new friends, and the boys attending new schools. For several years we spent money sending the boys to private schools, but that wouldn't be possible anymore. I was feeling grateful that my brothers, Steve and Joe both lived in the area. I knew this would help keep my loneliness at bay. Even though I always considered Boston my home, and I was leaving my parents there, I knew I had to make this change.

When morning came, I felt young again. I almost felt like a child at Christmas. My brother Joe was outside cleaning off his car and that morning we were going to see my future house. I was sure!

We drove through a few communities of homes where most of them were large and placed on nice lots. They looked like they were filled with families. Children's swing sets were covered in snow and everything looked peaceful, normal.

Joe drove down Delafield Drive. It was a tree-lined street that had been freshly plowed and halfway down he pulled into a wide driveway. Before us sat a massive two-story, 5-bedroom home. I was certain then. This was going to be my home.

Surprised by the enormous size of the house, Joe told me not to get my hopes up. It was too late for that. I reminded the boys to be polite and said a quick prayer before ringing the doorbell.

A woman opened the door with a big smile lighting up her face. As she welcomed us in and we greeted one another, my eyes darted around searching the rooms within. We went on a tour of the house and I was pleasantly surprised, almost overwhelmed, with the number of rooms it held. Even the basement was huge, with so much potential.

After the tour of this lovely house, we spoke in the kitchen. It took just a few moments for the owner to agree, despite my unemployed circumstance, to sign a one-year lease beginning January 01. I promised to have a security deposit and first month's rent by that time.

When I glanced over at my brother, he looked amazed. He didn't know how I pulled that off, but I guessed that he was happy for me. He was thrilled that the boys would be nearby, and he could be more a part of their lives going forward.

In my heart, I was sure there was some powerful meaning behind this transaction. I couldn't fathom that a woman I'd never met before had offered her home to my family and me when I didn't even have a job. It had to be a sign of good things to come. I knew I was supposed to move to Albany. I was in the right place, right where I was supposed to be.

# 04
## Chapter

## *Glimpse of God*

John remained at the Charles Street jail for two weeks. Because we didn't have the funds for a lawyer, he was assigned a public defender. With a possible twenty-year incarceration looming in his future, his next court date was scheduled for February 1$^{st}$, 1990.

John had friends in law enforcement, and they helped to have him moved from the lower levels that were infested with rats to a modular unit where inmates with affluent means were housed. As dim as his days were, this move brightened them a little.

After eight weeks at Charles Street, John was transferred to Bridgewater Addiction Center for a 28-day prison detox and rehabilitation program. Bridgewater was a medium security prison that John feared he wouldn't survive. I truly believe that had it not been for his past relationship with God, John would have stayed there a lot longer, perhaps twenty years. The entire church, Christian Assembly Church in Boston that is now located in Somerville, MA was praying for this. Mrs. Palma, pastor's wife, stood up with an easel at one Tuesday evening service and drew what looked like a clock. She asked for people of the congregation to sign up to say prayers for John. The congregation signed up a different person for every ten minutes of the day, around the clock. For a smaller-sized church, the support we received was amazing.

I reached out to John with information regarding another program that he, in turn, pursued. John was allowed to enter Teen Challenge, a Christian substance abuse recovery program. While the court had not previously heard of this program and the public defender dashed our hopes that it would be within the realm of possibility, things turned out in John's favor. On the day of sentencing, a representative unexpectedly attended the court proceedings that morning to speak on behalf of the program and advocate for allowing John to enter the program. We will be forever grateful to Dean Griffin for his assistance that day. To the surprise of the public defender and ourselves, the judge did indeed remand my husband to Dean Griffin and the Teen Challenge program's custody. As part of the sentencing, the judge stipulated that if John left the program prematurely, he would be remanded back to jail.

Since all of this was happening during the holiday season, John ended up spending his Christmas at Bridgewater. I didn't spend a lot of my time thinking about that. Looking back, it was really just a blessing that he wasn't spending the holiday, or any other day for that matter, still on the street. As a matter of fact, I'd told John previously that if he landed in jail, I would not visit him. I kept my word on that.

I was busy working through the major changes that were happening in my world. I really wasn't looking forward to talking with my parents when they returned from their trip. The boys and I gathered up what we needed to travel back to Brighton and my brothers planned to head back home as well. I was feeling very conflicted inside. Part of me was extremely excited about renting the new house in Albany and the other part of me was dreading the conversation I still had to have with my parents. I hadn't told them about the mess we suffered through at their house on Dec 8th or that I was taking the boys and moving three hours away.

When we were younger, John took me out to the suburbs of Boston and showed me beautiful houses where we could live. At the time, I couldn't imagine living outside of Brighton which I'd always thought of as home. Now, I was picking up and moving three hours away, to another state, with three kids no less. I wasn't the same woman he'd taken on that drive back then. I'd lived a lifetime since then.

My mind jumped around a lot on the trip back to Brighton. The distance gave me an opportunity to think about what I'd say to my parents. When it came right down to it, I wasn't really prepared for the conversation the way that it happened, but it was time to face the music.

We'd arrived late at night and I went straight to bed. I didn't think I'd see my folks until the next morning, but I was wrong. It wasn't long before I heard my mother coming down the stairs and I quickly pulled on my robe, meeting her by the back door. I could tell by the look on her face that she was upset. She knew something was wrong. Before I could say a word, she blurted out, "What happened while we were away?" She explained that she was catching up on mail and local news and spotted something in the police blotter that claimed John had been arrested for breaking into their house. She laid the paper out on the table as proof of her finding. This wasn't exactly how I'd planned the conversation, but I was knee-deep in it at that point.

I tried to explain the break-in to my mother, but how could I? It didn't make sense to me. I told her that he was hallucinating and that I really had no control over the situation. I don't think that helped to calm her at all. She was beside herself with emotions and I felt awful that I'd brought this mess to our family. She didn't hold back this time and I felt like her words were justified. She was right. She didn't want me or the kids to be anywhere near John in the future. It took me a long time to get there, but I fully agreed with her on that count.

After the sun came up, my father joined us in the kitchen of the downstairs apartment. As difficult as it was, I went through the events of the prior two weeks. Like my mother, he vented and expressed his concern over my welfare and that of the children. I listened in a way that I hadn't listened before. We even touched on the topic of divorce. While his words hurt, they were the truth.

With them both together, I told them of my plans to move to Albany. I explained that I'd escaped to New York after John's fiasco and spent the weekend with Joe. I told them that I felt the distance between John and I was a good thing and that I'd be staying there. The boys were excited about spending time with their uncles and I felt better about the decision knowing that my brothers would be close by to support me emotionally.

To say that my parents were shocked would be an understatement. Naturally, they wanted me away from John, but they didn't want me to fly that far from the nest. I think that at that moment if they could have prevented me from crossing the street, they would have. They were incredibly worried about me and my safety and couldn't see how they could care for me unless I was right under their noses. I understood and appreciated their concern, but I wasn't changing my mind.

I still hadn't told them that I'd signed a lease for a 5-bedroom house. I was afraid that might put them over the edge. I think they were afraid that if I was too far away, they couldn't prevent me from letting John back into my life. That wasn't my plan though. For the first time in my life, I felt strong enough to live without him. For the first time in my life, I felt strong, period. To help, I was reading the Bible daily at that point, gathering scripture to keep myself strong. Romans 8:28 "And we know that in all things God works for the good of those who love Him, who have been called according to His purpose."

I knew that the Holy Spirit was on my side. As long as I remained open and listened to the word of God, I would be safe. It wasn't that I didn't appreciate what my parents were offering to me, a job at the family restaurant and a place to live, but I knew that I had graduated in a way. I no longer had to rely on my parents to take care of my daily needs. By the power of God, I had the strength to begin taking care of myself.

I also didn't want my parents so closely involved in the drama caused by my broken marriage. They weren't getting any younger and I worried about their health. Now was time for me to stop relying on my parents or anyone else. By the power of God, I had the strength to begin taking care of myself and my boys. I had been talking about my newfound faith and now was time for me to act on it and walk the walk.

I thought of the verse from Jeramiah 29:11 which reads, "For I know the plans I have for you, declares the Lord. Plans to prosper you, not to harm you, plans to give you hope and a future. Then you will call upon me and pray to Me and I will listen. You will seek Me and find Me when you seek Me with all your heart." I repeated those words to myself whenever I felt doubt seeping in. I hadn't ever considered myself a strong person before. I had a lot to learn, but the good news was that I was open to receiving whatever lessons the Holy Spirit was about to teach me.

The boys went back to school in Brighton while I spent the next few days packing up their belongings. By the time Christmas week arrived, I had spent many sleepless nights worrying about how I was going to pay the rent on that beautiful, albeit huge, house in Albany.

I decided to head over to the garage that we still owned and talk to them about selling the whole thing. Up to this point, John had taken and sold bits and pieces, but I was going to need this money if I was going to make a go of it in Albany. There wasn't much negotiating that happened. I struck a deal to sell the business for a song and dance. When all was said and done, I had barely enough to pay the deposit on the house and 3 months' rent. Still, I was relieved. I smiled one of the few smiles that crossed my face that December and I immediately sent a check to Albany, making sure that house was mine and the boys' when we'd arrive in January.

I also made it a point to go to services and talk with Pastor Palma and his wife Phoebe. They had become an important part of my life. It all started after that fateful trip to the Bahamas. John came home with an itch to renew his relationship with God and just like that, God sent a friend to welcome him. Ed Carroll, his friend for years, invited John to join him at a Bible Study group at the home of Dr Viola at Crystal Lake in Newton, MA. That night, he met a group of people that explained what Jesus could do in his life. He told them about his problems with drugs and alcohol and that night he invited Jesus into his life. Admittedly, after even just one night I could see a positive change in John. He seemed happier and the peace within him just seemed to grow. He even started sleeping at night, which he hadn't done in a long while. He was attending Park St Church in Boston, MA with Ed Carroll on a regular basis.

When he described the experience to me, I was tempted to ask him if he was drunk. My husband sitting in a circle holding hands with these strangers and praying to Jesus. It was incomprehensible. When it had been his turn, John had asked Jesus to come back into his life and forgive his sins. From that point on, John felt like a new man. He said that he felt like 10,000 pounds had been lifted from his shoulders and he was at peace. He was born again and he wanted me to jump on the bandwagon with him. I was not willing to do that.

It took me a lot longer to renew my relationship with Christ. I dipped my toe in the water a few times, but in all honesty, I was still waiting for the other shoe to drop. I fought it for a while, but then one nondescript day, I felt a shift. It was that day when I realized that for so many years I'd been begging my husband to make a change when I was there with my own feet stuck in the mud. I was refusing to change myself. I didn't see a reason for me to change because I thought I was the "good one," but that day I'd become aware of the fact that I had a wall up about it.

After that, I became more open to the Word of God. I joined John's study group and began to really listen to the words spoken in our study group. The shared knowledge of the Bible impressed me and everyone was incredibly friendly. My mom mentioned to me one day that my grandmother read the Bible a lot and I remembered that when we were younger, my grandmother joined a Pentecostal Christian church. I thought maybe I could talk with her about it.

After months of coaxing by John and my grandmother, I decided to go to Sunday service with them. My Catholic upbringing had not prepared me for what I witnessed there. I found the service to be greatly uplifting and looked forward to going again. I was especially moved when John introduced me to Pastor Palma and Mrs. Palma for the first time and how they immediately welcomed me to the Church.

A few Sundays later, I stood by Mrs. Palma in the back of Church and asked Jesus to come into my life. I asked for forgiveness of my sins and I welcomed him as Lord and Savior of my life. Mrs. Palma told me that if I believed those words, then I was born again. I might have been born again in that moment, but I felt nothing at the time. Little by little, I was beginning to understand what it meant as I began to recognize Jesus in my everyday life more and more.

The day after welcoming Jesus in, I finally opened the beautiful gray Bible that John had given me. I slid my fingers over my name engraved on the cover and looked forward to the Word for the first time. Even though I'd opened the book many times over the preceding weeks, the words didn't resonate. This time, I was enraptured by what I was reading and couldn't put it down.

From there, John and I were baptized together. John was excited because the experience made him feel like he was getting a clean slate. I believed that being baptized together amongst family and friends would heal us forever. I was sure that it would wash away fear and anger, replacing it with peace forever. Only a few months had passed since our trip to the Bahamas, but right then, it felt like that awful experience had been a lifetime ago. In my mind, we'd been given the opportunity to begin a new life together, a life away from the sins of our past.

Unfortunately, evil tempted us much sooner than I'd expected. Later that same month, John was tested and failed. Without thinking it through. He purchased a dime bag of heroin at a random stop light in downtown Boston. It was in the form of a powder that he quickly sniffed up his nose. Within seconds, the peace that John had come to know and love evaporated. While John struggled with his relapse, I remained in the dark - again.

Brother Palma remained a cornerstone in our lives, and when he invited us to the convention in Washington for the Christian Church of North America (CCNA), we jumped at the opportunity. We flew down Labor Day weekend with our friends Ed and Suzanne Carroll. It was that weekend that I started to notice signs of John using again. I was appalled to think that he couldn't attend the conference without being high. He couldn't even make it through the weekend without a fix. Unbeknownst to me, John had hailed a cab and went downtown DC to purchase more Heroin. After he shot up, he headed back to the conference.

All that aside, the weekend had been enlightening and encouraging. Despite the fact that my marriage was eroding due to John's drug use again, I felt comforted by the messages delivered there. The fear that I'd felt at the beginning of the conference was beginning to be replaced with hope.

Next to me, during a worship service where the presence of God was profoundly felt, a man was praying in a different language that I'd never heard before. I remember looking over at him thinking it didn't sound like Italian, but Pastor Palma explained it was the Holy Spirit speaking through him. 1 Corinthians 14:14, "For if I pray in a tongue, my spirit is praying, but I don't understand what I'm saying."

After that service, I was compelled to find that man in the dispersing crowd. Tapping him on the shoulder when I spotted him, I said, "I was standing next to you during the service," but before I could finish my introduction, he interrupted me asking me if my name was Michelle.

Stunned, I confirmed that was indeed my name and he replied, "Please come over here and sit down with me. God gave me a word specifically for you." He proceeded to explain that one of the gifts of the

Holy Spirit, for those who believe, is the gift of the word of knowledge from God. I had never met this man before and yet he knew my name. Of course, I wanted to know what he had to say.

"I have been looking for you," he spoke softly. Now, this was really strange. I was astounded. He was looking for me, but we had never met. Nothing like this had ever happened to me before. With a firm handshake he said, "I'm Pastor Pat Bossio." He continued to share words that God had given him about me. He was to encourage me about making it through the tough times, or "deep waters," as he had called them. He referred to those I'd already navigated as well as those waters which I was about to enter. Pastor Bossio said, "as long as you listen to God's voice and fully trust him, peace will be restored. You need to be diligent about listening to God's voice through prayer, workshop, and reading the Bible. Be aware of that small voice during your prayer time with God. That is most often how He speaks; you will learn to know His voice. Michelle, the more that you understand God's ways and the closer you become to Him, the more you will understand how He communicates specifically to you. He does that for each of us who believe when we take the time to learn His ways and listen." Then he blew me away even further when he said, "God will restore your life and marriage and use it for a greater good." Romans 8:28, "And we know that in all things God works for the good of all who love Him, who have been called according to His purpose." Before disappearing into the large crowd of people gathering in the lobby, Pastor Bossio told me that he would continue to pray for my husband and for me. Looking back, Pastor Bossio had an immense impact on my life.

I quickly found Pastor Palma and he confirmed that the Holy Spirit had provided a message just for me and he was there to catch me when an incredible peace came over me. To the human eye, it would have looked like I'd passed out, but when I was touched by the Holy Spirit and fell backwards, I was aware of everything going on around me. Peace and contentment filled my entire being. The ceiling could have fallen in on me and I would not have cared.

I was going to need to lean on that peace in order to get me through what was in front of me. That rough and windy road had led to John being incarcerated and me sitting and explaining my relocation plans to my parents. Once they understood my plans to relocate and were fully on board, they assured me they'd keep an eye out for John.

Pastor Palma also told me that he had a friend who was a pastor in the Albany area. He promised to send his friend a note to let him know I was heading that way. I felt that sense of peace come over me again, knowing that Pastor Palma had a friend there.

As strong as I'd been feeling when Christmas Eve first rolled in, as the day started getting longer, I started thinking about John and his being apart from the boys on this holiday. I was starting to feel pretty sad about the whole situation. After everybody else left that night, my father came downstairs and sat on the couch with me. We talked about how difficult it was going to be on Christmas without John celebrating with us and just talking with him made me feel better. I knew that it was going to be ok.

I recalled what Pastor Bassio said to me in Washington. I would know God's voice. Like Hebrews 11:1 tells us, "Faith is the confidence that what we hope for will actually happen; it gives us assurance about things we cannot see." I had my faith and knew it would carry me through any difficulties I might encounter this holiday.

Christmas morning came and I was still feeling a little nervous about the changes I was making. I felt like I needed confirmation that I was still on the right path and so I decided to call Pastor Palma to see if I could stop by one more time before heading west in the morning. He invited me over that afternoon, and I picked up my cousin Susan Marie on the way. She'd just become a Christian herself and I wanted to see her before I left. On our way there, I mentioned to her that I needed a sign of some sort to reassure me. I'd never been away from my parents before and I hoped I was doing the right thing.

The Palmas greeted us with hugs and together we prayed for a safe move. We also prayed for my boys and their settling in nicely to the new home and routines. We had some coffee and then said our goodbyes.

When I was on the front steps, Pastor Palma stopped me and ran back into the house. He came out with a paper that had the information for his friend in Albany. When I read what was written on that piece of paper, my eyes glazed over with tears and I found it hard to speak. I couldn't believe what I was reading. The address for the Pastor's friend was on the same street where I was moving. Could that be right?

Sure enough, Pastor Gay's home was located directly across the street from my new home in Albany. Brother Palma was confident that this was the sign I had been seeking and I couldn't agree more.

Exuding confidence that I had previously been lacking, my mother took one look at me when I walked back through our front door and smiled. I told her about my new neighbor and she agreed that it was quite a coincidence. I knew that everything was falling into place and that I was on the right path. There are no coincidences.

# 05
## Chapter

## Making New York Home

The next morning finally arrived. It was moving day. My parents, aunts, brothers, and cousins were all there to support me. All those hands helping me to pack the truck made it quick work. In addition to all our belongings, we made room for the fifteen bags of food and supplies that, to my surprise, the Christian Assembly Church dropped off for us two days before. In no time at all, we were ready to hit the road.

Just as I was closing the door to my apartment, I heard the phone ringing. Without our belongings filling the space, the ring echoed much louder in my ear. I surmised that John was on the other end of the line that morning. I considered answering but decided against it. I didn't want to make what was already an emotional morning worse. I closed the door and locked it behind me. I was determined to be strong, even with tears stubbornly streaming down my cheeks.

My brother Joe was sitting in the driver's seat of the moving truck waiting for me. I gathered up the boys as the rest of my family headed to their own vehicles. Everyone was heading to Albany now. I'm sure it must have looked like a parade with my convoy of support. These folks helped me all my life. I was blessed to have them. For a moment, I thought of John sitting alone in jail with no family left to support him. I didn't let it stop me because I knew my future was in another state.

We arrived in Albany, all seven vehicles. While the boys played in the yard at our new house, my family helped me carry in the boxes where I'd placed all my worldly possessions. Together we arranged all the furniture and they even helped me hang pictures on the blank walls. There was a spot for everything we brought. My cousins Susan Marie and Suzanna lined my kitchen cabinets and filled them with my dishes. By evening, everyone had a place to sleep in the huge house, even if it was just mattresses spread across the floors. My body ached from exhaustion. Still, sleep was evasive. My thoughts were scattered.

I found myself thinking of John and how we'd gotten to this point. I remembered the first time that I actually sat down with the Bible and read it, really read it. I was really thankful for Ed's wife Suzanne. We used to talk on the phone every day and she answered a lot of questions I had. I'd ask her questions about what I was reading in the Bible and I'd also use her for a sounding board where John was concerned.

In my mind, I even went back to the Bahamas; sitting in that hotel room was the first time that I asked God to make Himself real to me and the first time I felt like He was listening to me. John and I even had weekly Bible studies at our home. I remember my dad telling me after one meeting that listening to our friends brought him peace and that when we read and prayed in our home, there was a different feeling in the air.

It was that peace I desperately needed in my life now. For so long, John had told me he would stop drinking and using drugs, but somewhere along the way, after the disappointment of so many failed attempts, I'd just stopped trusting him. His life was in God's hands now and I was comforted by Roman's 5:8 "But God shows His love for us in that while we were still sinners, Christ died for us." I understood that Jesus died on the cross for all His people, not just for the "good" ones. I let go of my trying to control the situation and turned it over to God.

After that conference in Washington, John fell into the routine of spending his hard-earned cash on drugs. He'd disappear for days at a time. As his drug habit grew, his business success and our money evaporated. He went from spending all his free time with me when we were dating to spending most of his time away from me, stroking his addiction to drugs. His friends became those who supplied him his next fix.

John chose to downsize his automotive repair business, moving to a smaller garage with fewer employees. It was then I took stock of the clothes and jewelry that had become a surrogate for the love I'd been missing in my marriage. I wasn't worried about losing ready access to all the glitz and glamor. I would have traded all the material treasures in a heartbeat to have John free of his addictions and engaged in the boys' and my life. We had lived in the home that John had grown up in and purchased from his father's estate.

From there, we moved back into my parent's home, taking the first-floor apartment. It was then that John started missing services at church. He told me it was because he had to work extended hours at the garage, but I knew better. I tried to maintain my trust that God had everything under control because I knew I surely didn't. What really scared me was when John told me that he'd lost the peaceful feeling that he got from being in relationship with Jesus. He said he just couldn't get back to the comfort of the Holy Spirit. I knew something was really wrong then, but I kept making excuses to our friends for his absence from church services.

John kept sinking deeper, so low that I hardly recognized him. I guessed those were the days signified by the deep waters that Pastor Bossio had forewarned me of. I could still hear a small voice guiding me through the treacherous waters, but I didn't know how long I could hold on to that.

He told me much later that he was sitting at a traffic light and the thought came over him to do a bag of heroin. This is the insanity of addiction. After all that he had experienced with God, he made the decision to go and buy a bag. Which he did. As soon as the heroin touched his nose, he lost every sense of peace that he had gained.

I lost some of my peace too. It was difficult for me with John being out until all hours doing who knows what. I was virtually raising three boys alone. They were and still are my pride and joy. When I became depressed, the boys always gave me the courage to go on. Before, courage came by the way of money, shopping and new cars. I developed a habit that gave me an escape. Shopping was my coping mechanism.

When John would show up, I felt angry and frustrated. I was ready to explode, but I held everything in. I had held everything in since the day we met, thinking it was the right thing to do. At first, I thought John's behavior was my fault. I wasn't a good enough wife. Then, I came to realize that it didn't matter what I did; John was following his own path. No matter how many times he promised to quit, he slipped further and further back into his old habits.

I prayed with my pastor and the time came when I knew I had no choice. I had to tell John to move out. I didn't want the boys subject to his unstable behavior anymore. I didn't want to deal with it anymore. There was no more business. The accountant came by and told me that John had been selling pieces of it off and now owed more to lenders than was coming in.

Once I'd made up my mind, I waited for John to surface again. Then, I told him he was no longer welcome in our home. My legs were weak, and I thought I'd never stop crying, but I held firm. After nine years of marriage, I had no idea how I was going to take care of the boys, but I knew I had no choice. I worked with the accountant and sold the business. I'm not sure John even noticed.

I kept leaning on the things I learned at the conference in Washington. I felt God's reassurances and remembered Pastor Bossio's words which led me to an unexpected calmness, gave me a reason to keep putting one foot in front of the other, and filled me with hope. I counted on our lives being restored so that we could one day fulfill a greater purpose. I remember reading Jeremiah (29:11): "For I know the plans I have for you, declares the Lord, plans for welfare (good) and not for evil, to give you a future and a hope." I was learning that the Bible is a gift from God to guide us all through life. It is the anointed word of God. I found myself in every situation; when I opened it up, the words gave me peace and direction.

Those words continued to help me in what was now my new home in New York. I finally nodded off to sleep and by the next morning, a plan was forming in my mind. I went downstairs and my cousin Susan Marie had also come down. I asked her to join me on a trip across the street to meet Pastor Gay and his family. Pastor Gay was the man that

Pastor Palma had told me about when we talked in Boston of my move to New York. It was a cold winter day; I bundled up my youngest, Daniel and together the three of us ventured out.

When my neighbor's door opened, I was invited into Pastor Gay's home. His wife, Joyce who had been busy baking in the kitchen, rushed out to also welcome my youngest son Daniel and me to the neighborhood. Their daughter, Anita, was also there and welcome us in.

I couldn't wait to share my experience with them. I told them how his friendship with Brother Palma and his now being my neighbor was a sign for me. How it affirmed that I was following the Holy Spirit's guidance and how much comfort this gave me. With our brief conversation, I could already tell that we were going to have a close, meaningful relationship and I was confident that we would bond just like I had with Brother Palma.

I didn't realize it then, but we had already met once before. Pastor Gay was at the National Christian Conference in Washington, DC. that I'd attended the year before, after John had moved out.

John and I pretty much lived apart for two years before he was arrested that night in December. The first year, he'd struggled with drug abuse, drug programs, hospitals, counseling, police and many unanswered questions. I had no idea from one day to the next where he would be; jail, rehab, on the streets, or in the morgue.

Once he was gone from the house, I still worried about him, especially in the winter months without a home and I hoped deep inside that John could change. He called me frequently from pay phones, but after a while, I stopped answering. Every conversation ended with me screaming at him to get help and I was getting nowhere. My feelings for him had turned from love to hate to anger and pity.

Leading up to that trip a year ago, the weather was harsh with the news reporting the falling snow would soon turn into freezing rain. Prior to the trip John called asking me to bring his dress suit to him. I didn't know what he wanted it for, but at the time it seemed like a positive sign. He was still the love of my life and I wanted to help him. This was something simple I could do, leave his suit in an unlocked car at his garage for him, and could do it without bringing the rest of my family into the drama. This would be my second trip to the CCNA convention.

John was supposed to have gone with me, but that didn't work out. I didn't know how he was going to do it, but he still planned on attending.

Two days later, I forgot about the suit and John's intention to attend the conference. I left my boys under the watchful care of my mother and cousin and headed to the Crystal Gate Marriott in Washington, DC with friends Ed and Suzanne and cousin Susan Marie. Pastors and their wives, along with the leaders of churches throughout the country would be gathering. I was really hoping to gain strength and perhaps a miracle at the conference, not only for me but for John too.

The first morning of the conference, while I was listening to a tremendous speaker, Lillian Sparks, I could hear a commotion outside the door. I tried to ignore it, but it just continued. When I looked up at the door again, I saw my friend Ed motioning for me to come over. I hesitated because the speaker was so good but eventually made my way over.

When I got outside the door, I spotted Pastor Palma and knew immediately that something was wrong by the look on his face. Ed let me know that John had arrived and was resting in the hotel lobby. When we got downstairs, we saw John sleeping in a chair in the lobby. He had brought two bags and his suit was carefully placed on the arm of the chair.

It was sad to see him sleeping there. He really did look homeless, like a child with no place to go. My heart broke right then and there. Pastor Palma arranged for a room for John and suggested that I not get involved. I took Pastor Palma's advice and went back to the conference.

I was very upset and my nerves were shot. Thankfully, I received a tremendous amount of support from those attending the conference with me. It wasn't until later in the day that I saw John again. We both attended the evening service and John sought out my company. He found his way to the seat next to me and sat down in the suit that I'd dropped off for him. He looked much better, but I could tell he was uncomfortable. Pastor Palma and Ed watched over him as the service went on. Reverend Schambach spoke at service, which was very dynamic, and his words were very inspiring. At the end of service, they did an altar call where John went up to the altar by himself. Although he didn't know John, through the Holy Spirit imparting a word of knowledge to him, Reverend Shambach went over to John and in his powerful voice prayed the words, "I transfuse you with the blood of Jesus Christ and rebuke the spirit of addiction from you." He continued to pray for the complete deliverance from addiction and for protection from evil. Referencing 2 Corinthians 5:17, he told John that he was now a new creature in Christ and that the old man had passed away.

People from the conference had joined hands making a circle around my husband. My eyes filled with tears as I stood back and watched. Everyone surrounding John began to pray and I thought to myself, God is working miracles in our lives. John had made it to the conference which very much surprised me and I'm not easily surprised. It was an unbelievable weekend. I never experienced compassion and concern from others like this before. I truly felt the love of God from these people.

# 06
## Chapter

*Falling Into Place*

My family left later that afternoon. We shared hugs, kisses and well wishes. My mother cried a lot. She was going to miss my boys tremendously and this separation was going to be difficult. My heart ached with hers. It was a smaller convoy that left the drive. I was staying behind with my boys. I was in a new house, in a new neighborhood. I was beginning an entirely new life.

The boys and I walked back inside the house. I was amazed that the move was complete. There was nothing left to unpack or put away. All we had left to do now was go food shopping.

I opened my wallet and counted $200. That was all the money I had left. We grabbed our coats and went out to get food and supplies.

That Monday morning, winter break was over and I enrolled the boys in school. Daniel would be staying home with me. That first Sunday, the four of us attended services at our new church. The congregation was friendly and welcoming.

My children were like magnets to new friends. Church and school were two places that offered me new friendships as well. When the boys played outside or we went out for walks in the neighborhood, I also met more people.

Daniel loved playing in the snow. The crunching of his boot on the snow seemed to give him confidence. The boys adjusted well to the move, but still noticed little differences. One thing that jumped out at them was how our new neighborhood didn't have sidewalks.

I'm not sure exactly how it happened, but the children also led me to my source of income. I wasn't the only one needing help. Lots of my new friends needed help too and in a way that I could benefit. My love of children and their need for childcare seemed like a perfect fit, a win-win situation.

Staring out my living room window feeling empowered, I knew that if I did anything here, it would happen here with Daniel. By the time I walked away from that window, I knew that my skills as a mother qualified me to open a daycare. The house we lived in now gave me plenty of room to make that happen.

I wrote a short piece for the paper and within six weeks I had a waiting list and two assistants. I was able to hire two women from my new church and was happy to hear that they could start right away. Once again, the provision of God was at work. I got licensed by the state for a group family daycare which allowed me to have up to 14 children at a time.

Things were falling into place, but my thoughts were still racing. I still suffered many sleepless nights and battled unsettling nightmares. I knew John was still out there. I sent him a note that included a PO Box in Albany where he could send me letters if he felt compelled to communicate. I wasn't ready to speak with him yet and continually doubted his ability to recover from drug addiction but did encourage him to break the chain of addiction his family had created. I encouraged him to trust in God again and let Him light the way. My belief was that the Lord had taken John out of my hands so that He could work with him Himself. That wasn't necessarily what John believed. My letters to John, not frequent in the beginning, included scripture aimed at helping him get free from his addiction. Each of my letters ended with Proverbs 29:1,

"A man who remains stiff-necked after many rebukes will suddenly be destroyed – without remedy." It was time for John to pay attention.

I was afraid that John might be discouraged by the length of the Teen Challenge program. The program took place over a 12–15-month period. John barely made it through 2 weeks in the past. I told him in my letter that if he chose jail instead of the Teen Challenge, I wouldn't let him see me or the kids again. He'd be out of our lives forever. It was going to be his choice, but we were all going to have to live with the consequences.

About six weeks after sending John the PO box, I woke up feeling differently about the situation. I felt for the first time in a long time that I'd like to hear from my husband. My brother passed the post office on a regular basis and agreed to stop that day on his way home from work to check for a letter from John. Even though my husband wasn't an avid writer and I had no expectations that he would actually use that PO box, a letter was waiting for me.

My nerves got the best of me when I opened that letter and I wasn't sure what I'd find in the envelope. To my surprise, John seemed to have a clear mind when he put pen to paper, apologizing for the things that he had done and even accepting all the blame for his actions. There was no hint of my being at fault for any of his troubles, which was quite unusual.

I had told him in the few letters that I had sent to contact Team Challenge on his own. It was required that John make the effort himself to get into the program as they only accept people that have a desire to be there and get help.

After receiving the letter from John, I called the jail, hoping to speak with John's caseworker. I wanted to pass along information regarding forms necessary for applying to Teen Challenge. John also needed a physical prior to being admitted.

I called the office several times throughout the day, but the number was consistently busy. It wasn't until mid-afternoon that the caseworker finally answered. She listened to the outstanding tasks that John needed to take care of and then surprised me by letting me know that my husband was actually sitting in her office at that very moment. She said it was very unusual, but since he was in the office, she asked if I wanted to speak with him.

She handed the phone to John and I didn't know what to say. Earlier that morning I'd had a desire to speak with my husband but never thought it would actually happen. I wasn't really prepared to talk with him. Since I was speechless on my end, John began talking to me. Incredibly, he sounded just like he used to. He was reassuring me that he was going to recommit his life to the Lord and would do everything in his power to get into the Teen Challenge program. Regardless of how our marriage ended up, John was determined to serve God.

After a few minutes, John asked me how I was feeling and the words sounded very sincere. I still wasn't sure of my voice and remained silent. John went on to tell me that he'd been praying to God about healing our relationship. He was hopeful that one day I would welcome him back into my life. He knew now wasn't the time, but he was going to work hard to make that happen.

John kept up the one-sided conversation for a while, but as the call was coming to a close, I did finally say a few words. I told him that if he was successfully admitted into the teen challenge program and successfully completed the first 60 days of the program, I would consider heading to Boston for a visit with him.

I hung up the phone feeling more confused than ever. I was somewhat encouraged by John's words. At the same time, I'd heard him commit to change in the past, many times. He'd attempted rehab 8 different times. How would this time be any different?

# 07
## Chapter

## Trusting God

When John's court date arrived, I was astonished to learn that the home invasion charge had been dropped. I was also surprised to hear the judge approved John's attending the in-house treatment program known as Teen Challenge. It looked like John's hard work had paid off and he was a getting break.

There were a lot of rules and regulations that John was going to have to abide by at Teen Challenge. For starters, the judge insisted that John remain on campus for 12 months and complete this program. If he left the center before completion, he'd be picked up by the police and be incarcerated for two years. In addition to four hours of Bible study each morning, John was going to have to work while he was there. This wasn't a free pass for John.

I was glad that I had the activity of preparing for my new daycare center to occupy my thoughts. I wasn't ready to think about visiting with John again.

Even so, memories of my past continued to haunt me. John's abuse of both alcohol and drugs broke my heart and almost my soul. Often, I'd run down the list of reasons why John ended up where he was. He started drinking and smoking long before I had entered his life. I was just too naïve to know better.

I wasn't sure how moving to another state fit into our broken marriage. I wasn't sure if it was going to help or hurt. I just knew that I had to do what I had to do and trusted God to take care of the rest.

Pastor Gay's wife, Joyce, stopped me after service one Sunday and let me know that she was praying for John. She told me that even though she didn't know him personally, she felt a spiritual connection with him. She was confident that when he came to New York to live, that hundreds of people would come to know Christ because of him and his testimony of God's restorative power.

I wasn't sure what to think about Joyce's message to me. In my mind, I hadn't really thought about John coming to New York. Others at church also talked to me, trying to encourage and tell me that John would be joining me in Albany. I wasn't even sure I wanted that. I hadn't moved forward with an official separation or even considered divorce yet. That was mostly because I didn't have the funds to make any of that happen.

Just thinking about seeing John was unsettling. My life was finally getting stability. My boys were settling into their new routines nicely. I couldn't think about John being a part of my life again and disturbing this newfound peace and balance.

I had 60 days to figure out how to fit John into a small compartment in my life. I knew I couldn't open myself up completely to him again. It was too soon. I did want to be supportive, as long as he was making smart choices and doing the work. I would visit him and start writing letters again.

I began writing occasional letters to John. I gave him no inkling of reconciliation between us. My writing probably seemed a bit standoffish to him, but it was important to me to stick to the seriousness of our situation. I did not want to lead John to think there was hope for us to get back together at that time. Regardless of that, I didn't want to be a hindrance to his recovery and wanted to encourage him along his healing path.

# 08
## Chapter

## *Not Alone*

The weeks that followed were full of preparation for the grand opening of my daycare. I was once again blessed by God. Many neighbors and fellow parishioners shared their gently used toys with me. By the time opening day was upon me, I had a basement full of tricycles, big wheels, and ageless Fisher Price toys. I even managed to find a child-sized picnic table to serve lunches. I even got permission from my landlord to build child-sized cubbies for the children to store their belongings. I set up cribs, playpens and swings. I had everything I needed to begin a new career.

All of this activity kept my mind from obsessing about John virtually under house arrest at Teen Challenge. I had ruminated on his drug and alcohol addiction for many years. Now, it was time to focus on my own life. It was time for me to go after my own goals.

There was no doubt that some things would have been easier if John was there with me. For one thing, he'd have been able to build those cubbies in no time. I was sure, however, that there'd have been tradeoffs.

For every positive way that John could have helped me, there were 10 more ways that he'd bring grief and instability to my life.

While I wasn't sure that I was completely giving up on John and our marriage, I knew that I wasn't ready to let him back into my life in any significant manner either. John wasn't the only one benefiting from this time apart. While he was healing wounds and learning to manage his addictions at Teen Challenge, I had the opportunity to get to know myself. I was finding out who Michelle Mulledy really was, finding out what I was really capable of.

For so many years, I was just an extension of John. For the first time in my life, I was coming into my own. I was standing on my own two feet. I was scared, but I was even more determined. The tenacity that kept me believing in John all those years was finally kicking in where I could believe in myself. It might have been a subtle shift, but it had a significant impact on my life.

Not for a second did I think I was doing this by myself. I knew with every fiber of my being that the Holy Spirit was my teacher. God was lighting my path and leading me out of darkness. My husband wasn't with me, but I wasn't alone.

I was learning how to trust. I trusted God to care for me and watch over me. I trusted myself to make the best decisions. This was new for me, but it was so very empowering.

Yes, that's it. I was learning how to become powerful. I was no longer handing my power over to my husband and to his addictions. Instead, I was realizing the power bestowed upon me through the Holy Spirit to fulfill my dreams.

Before I knew it, opening day arrived and cars filled the driveway. I made sure to greet each parent and child, welcoming them and making them feel comfortable. During the mornings and afternoons, I'd focus on the children, singing and playing with them. I even tried to teach them things like their letters and numbers. All the things that I worked on with my own boys.

At the end of the day, however, I found myself often comforting their parents. When it first started happening, I was surprised, but after a while, it seemed more like a calling. As young parents shared their troubles with me, I began to pray with them. Like Ed Carroll touching

John's life and subsequently mine by sharing the good Word with us, I was bringing the Word to these families. I never expected this type of ministry to be part of my service when I opened the daycare, but I trusted that God knew best how I should share my gifts.

Still, there were times when I found myself wanting to listen to my head instead of trust divine guidance. One particular instance was when a young lady called asking to enroll her two boys in my daycare. I immediately explained to her that I had reached my capacity and wasn't accepting any more children into the program. I offered to place her name on a waiting list and call her as soon as something opened up again.

Like the parents who shared their stories with me and now prayed with me, this woman began to tell me her story. She had two boys, one newborn. The little one was born with complications. He had to stay in the hospital for days after birth while he was supplied 100% oxygen. She explained that the doctors weren't sure if he'd suffered lasting brain damage and it was all a very stressful time.

I found myself being drawn by the woman's story. I asked how the baby was now and was relieved to hear that the doctors had recently given her son a clean bill of health and even went so far as to call it a miracle. I really wasn't surprised to hear that God had worked yet another miracle. I was coming to expect this in my life now.

Oddly enough, I felt compelled to share my own story with this woman. Kim was her name. I told Kim about my situation and the circumstances that led me to opening up the daycare that she so desperately wanted her boys in. I spoke of the addictions that plagued my marriage and told her that my husband had been arrested and was currently living at a Christian men's center in another state.

Neither of us were used to sharing such intimate details of our lives with strangers, but we really didn't feel like strangers. Instead, there was an immediate connection. I knew I was talking to someone that God had placed on my path and I looked forward to meeting and getting to know her better. I invited her to come over the next day and we'd figure things out together.

The next day Kim arrived at my house with her two boys. She introduced her older son, Sean, and handed her little one, Corey to me. Bringing these boys into my daycare felt right to me. I knew that it was meant to be and that it would work out fine.

What I didn't expect was that each day when Kim would bring her boys and pick them up from my house, she'd also ask me about my faith. She wanted to know what gave me my strength. Before long, she came to service with me and I had the honor of praying alongside her as she welcomed Jesus into her life. It worked out so well that Kim ended up joining me working at my daycare and being able to spend the days with her children too.

That wasn't the only experience I had like this. God surely works in mysterious ways. Valeria was another mom who's twin girls were enrolled at my daycare. We often chatted at the end of the day, but I was pleasantly surprised when Valeria called me one morning to talk about something other than the children. She wanted to know more about the Christian faith and what it really meant to be a Christian.

I shared with Valeria my thoughts and feelings on what it meant to be a Christian and to walk in the light of God. I spoke of service and sharing our gifts, but I also talked about trusting God to take care of us. Perhaps even more meaningful to her was the inner peace that I described.

I asked Valeria if she wanted to join me at service and she jumped at the opportunity. It wasn't long after that she accepted Jesus into her life too. From there, she accepted the position of church secretary. It felt like I was making a difference in people's lives.

Another woman, a neighbor I was forging a new friendship with, stopped by the house after an upsetting visit she had with her doctor. She was diagnosed with breast cancer and was scheduled for surgery. I prayed for her and invited her to join a Bible study that I was hosting in my home that evening. She came back to my house that evening and our group prayed for her healing. One woman in particular told me that she felt strongly that I was to pray over my friend. I was reminded of a similar happening at a prayer group a few weeks prior when another woman told me that she believed that God had graced me with the gift of healing. I wasn't sure about that, but in all honesty, I did feel compelled to pray over my new friend.

I placed my hands on her shoulders and began praying out loud. This was new for me and I felt a little uncomfortable at first. Then, it was almost like something shifted and I leaned into it. I didn't have to think about what to say or do; the words just came naturally to me. I prayed over my friend and felt alive, clear and connected. I couldn't explain it and really, putting it into words is somewhat difficult, but I definitely felt as though I was standing in the flow of God's love.

When I finished, my friend turned and told me that she'd never experienced anything quite like that before. She said that she felt an incredible heat from my hands, and she felt a warm peace filling her being. She felt much calmer than she had when she arrived at my house and was very grateful for the prayers that I'd said over her.

I wasn't sure how to handle this new experience. I didn't know how it fit into my life, but I couldn't deny that it felt wonderful. It felt like I was connected to something bigger than me. I was connected to God and was now connecting to my community. I was a little overwhelmed by this. It certainly wasn't something I expected and I wasn't sure what to do with it, but I knew it was something positive.

My friend had more tests and they found that her cancer required only a lumpectomy rather than the mastectomy she had feared. Chemotherapy also could be avoided. We were both very excited about this news and I had no doubt that this positive turn was due to God's intervention. It seemed that He used me to bring this woman to receive His healing grace. I was humbled to know that I might have been a party to God's work in this way.

If I was to believe this and accept this, I'd be acknowledging that somehow through all of the pain and despair in my life, God had blessed me with an incredible gift. I thought of Isaiah 61:3 who said, "to bestow on them a crown of beauty instead of ashes, the oil of gladness instead of mourning, and a garment of praise instead of a spirit of despair."

I was encouraged that God chose me to spread His word. I felt like my life had a purpose. I had no doubt that anything was possible with the Lord in my life.

# 09
## Chapter

## *Head On*

While I'd like to say those first days in Albany were all glory days, that wasn't the case. I enjoyed the peace in my soul a good deal of the time, but there were still plenty of times that my mind raced. I knew that these thoughts I gave in to on a daily basis were not fostered by God but were harbored by my mental weakness and fears. Fear had become something that I was dealing with on a daily basis. To cope with the fear I kept praying to God and reading the Bible where I was reminded, "For God did not give us the spirit of fear, but of power and of love, and of a sound mind. "2 Timothy 17. I repeated that scripture again and again each day.

I was given to many sleepless nights filled with relentless nightmares. It didn't matter that I had made so much progress in my life. It didn't matter that I'd built something more stable than I'd experienced in all of my adult years. It didn't matter that I spent most of my waking hours tending to this new life, focusing on ways to ensure peace and security for my boys and me. After years of living with an addict, doubt had taken residence in my subconscious and wasn't letting go.

**Addicted To Hope**

I decided to voice my doubts, my concerns. I hoped that this action would give me the release that I needed. I wrote John a letter at Teen Challenge:

*February 1990*

*Dear John,*

*I have to tell you that I have been having the worst nightmares of my life. Every time I close my eyes, I start dreaming about our past. I don't know why this is coming back to me at night, but it has been happening a lot. I am remembering so many details. These dreams are right out of Hell!*

*All I know is that I have been a good and faithful wife to you. I took our marriage seriously. Maybe there are things about you that I couldn't see. I thought you had a good heart but were confused about life. Basically, I thought we both wanted the same things.*

*I know that I truly loved you. I don't want to think of my husband as simply a person to wait on or a man who only comes home when he feels like it. One thing this experience has shown me is that I deserve more than someone who treats me like a doormat. I never treated you that way, ever.*

*Every day I have couples dropping off their kids at my daycare. I see the way these guys value what they have with their wives and kids. They may not have much materially, but they love and trust each other. They would never treat their family with such little respect as you did.*

*I want my husband to treat me the same way as these couples I see every day; to be part of the family all the time, not only when you feel like it. Your idea of marriage right now is downright disgusting and so far from being a man that it is sad. The Bible says, "An excellent wife, who can find? She is far more precious than jewels." (Proverbs 31:10).*

*Well, the kids and I were the good part of your life that has been taken away from you. Luckily for you, John, God gives second chances. I still have love for you, but if you want to completely change, you know who can do that for you — Jesus, God's son! If you are still being deceptive and putting on an act, then it is only a matter of time before you totally destroy yourself. I hope and pray that doesn't happen. You have a lot going for you and God could use you in a big way. I'm praying every day that God will reveal Himself to you. Get rid of the evil stuff inside and see the real John Mulledy. Take off the old man and put on the new man — a new being in Christ.*

*God has outdone Himself providing for our children and me. I don't know if you are willing to give me what I want. What you do at Teen Challenge will show how you really feel. I don't care what happens there; if you leave the program, it's over – DIVORCE! You can make it if you try and if you want a new life badly enough. I'll never go back to the way things were. No more having things "only your way." It is God's way or nothing.*

*I'll be there to see you when I need to. This is your last chance. Otherwise, I stay alone for good. It is up to you.*

*Michelle*

*PS Call Joe's office if you need to contact me. The kids love you. Remember, they deserve a father that cares. I know you do!*

Wow. I felt so much better after writing that letter. I didn't know how John would feel when he received it, but I felt like I'd finally said what was bubbling inside me for years. I guessed it was about time that I started paying attention to my own feelings and honoring myself. I'd spent so much time worrying about John's feelings and caring for him and the boys that I really hadn't paid attention to myself.

For the first time in my life, I was speaking my truth, not just about my new life but about the life I'd left behind in Massachusetts. For years, I hadn't shared my story. I hadn't even spoken to my parents about the lonely, chaotic life that I'd led. Now was the time, however. There was no question in my mind. I was going to face these doubts, these fears, head on. I was going to own them and honor them. It wasn't like they were unfounded. How many times had I been let down by my husband, the man I was supposed to trust most in this world.

My challenge now was to build a life that couldn't be harmed by John's reckless behavior. I couldn't control John, but I could control the chaos that I allowed into my life. I hoped that he took my letter seriously enough. There was no way that I would allow him to wreak havoc on my life again. I knew now what it was like to live a stable life. I knew what it was like to have a supportive community around me. I knew what it was to accept Jesus and His Holy Spirit into my life.

No one, not John or anyone else was ever going to take me back to the nightmare that used to be my way of life. I was rewriting my story and if he wanted to be a part of it, John was going to have to rewrite his story too.

The response I got from John was brief. I had bared my soul to him and he responded by asking for writing supplies and a few articles of clothing. I'm not sure what I was expecting, but it certainly would have felt better if he'd at least acknowledged my pain. To say I was disappointed was an understatement. It was yet another let down sustained at my husband's hand.

Who was this man that I still called my husband? Who had he become? Was he so self-absorbed that he didn't even pretend to care about my feelings now? Our marriage had always been centered around taking care of his needs, but I was changing. In addition to caring for our children, I was awakening to my own needs and if he wanted to be a part of my life, he was going to have to change too.

# 10
## Chapter

# Teen Challenge

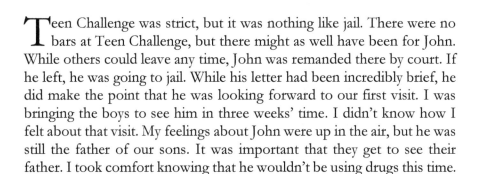

Teen Challenge was strict, but it was nothing like jail. There were no bars at Teen Challenge, but there might as well have been for John. While others could leave any time, John was remanded there by court. If he left, he was going to jail. While his letter had been incredibly brief, he did make the point that he was looking forward to our first visit. I was bringing the boys to see him in three weeks' time. I didn't know how I felt about that visit. My feelings about John were up in the air, but he was still the father of our sons. It was important that they get to see their father. I took comfort knowing that he wouldn't be using drugs this time.

The next few letters that I received from John were up and down. One letter spoke of his desire to run away from the program. I was shocked and hurt when I read that letter. He was obviously struggling. I spoke to Jim Vitale, the director of the program who was known to the students as Jimmy V., and he told me that John's behavior was very typical of addicts. He seemed to be focusing on when he'd come home and I wasn't ready to talk about that then. Once again, emotions were running very high between the two of us.

He did follow up the letter about abandoning the program with another one that said he couldn't be dragged away from the program. This time he swore that he was going to complete the program and couldn't wait to be reunited with his family. To say that he was on an emotional roller coaster was putting it lightly. Each time I received a letter, I had to remind myself to not read too much into it. He didn't have a handle on his emotions yet. He was receiving counseling while he was at Teen Challenge. The difference with Teen Challenge was that the people running it, including the director, were former addicts. They were able to spot when someone was lying or just giving lip service. They also had a meeting with the staff each morning where they'd pray for each student enrolled in the program. I was very thankful for their counsel and their integration of the spiritual aspect of recovery.

I was so thankful that John was at Teen Challenge and not living in my house right now. I thought about my daily routine, getting the boys off to school and then welcoming those children into my daycare, sometimes attending prayer service in the evening, talking with new friends that I'd made. My life was so much calmer and I truly enjoyed it that way. I was no longer spending endless hours wringing my hands, wondering where my husband was and what would happen next. I was able to release those worries to God now. I could concentrate on my boys. Such a heavy burden had been lifted. I tried to think of the good times we'd had over the years and focus less on the bad times.

On a positive note, it did sound like he was finding his way back to Christ. There were notes of renewed passion for the Holy Spirit and I found that very encouraging. I could only hope that over time, the grace of God would spread over to other areas of John's life.

It seemed like all I could do for my husband right now, all that I wanted to do, was listen to his vents, his confessions, and pray for him. I would send words of encouragement only. My notes reminded him that he was the only one that could make this time count. He was the only one that could successfully complete the program and become the man that he was meant to be. It wasn't my job to hold his feet to the fire every day and I let him know that. It was his responsibility. I knew that he missed his sons, but if he wanted to be back in his boys' lives again, he was going to have to be accountable for his actions and get through this. He had to successfully follow this program through to the end.

John's mood swings, the ups and downs he displayed in his letters, left me swinging too. From one day to the next, I just wasn't sure what to believe or what to trust. I couldn't really imagine ever fully trusting John again, not with day to day things and especially not with my heart. Only time would tell.

One positive thing John shared with me back then was that he got a job at Teen Challenge. He was assigned to take care of the automobiles in the garage there. He sounded elated when he wrote about that. For the first time in a long time, I think he felt like he could contribute again, add value. Maybe this job was giving him back a sense of his manhood. I was hopeful that this assignment could be a turning point for him. I just didn't let my hopes rise too much.

He wrote me just about every day. Sometimes he sent two letters in one day. He was also allowed one call a week. The calls were short and I wanted to make sure that he spoke to each of the boys. I admit that it was nice to hear his voice. On some level I was comforted, but I didn't allow myself to believe the things that he told me. I couldn't believe his promises anymore. It was a painful lesson, but I'd learned it. John couldn't be trusted.

At some point, his letters started to mention coming to New York. He talked about a Teen Challenge program in the state and he even asked about the house where the boys and I lived. He wanted me to send more pictures of the boys and me. He asked for pictures of the house too! I felt like he was beginning to intrude on my new life. How dare he think he can just walk into my life and my home again, just like that.

I knew that he was still my husband, but I wasn't sure how much I could honor the promises we'd made. I certainly wasn't looking for anyone else. If I wasn't with John, I'd be raising the boys alone. It was going to be a difficult choice, but that was the choice I had to make. In prayer, when considering the move to New York, I promised myself and the Lord that I would serve God no matter what happened between John and I.

I knew that if I chose to walk away, John would be in total shock. For all of my married life, I'd centered my whole life around John and the boys. I'd considered him in every decision I'd made and every action I'd taken. I can understand why he'd think that the future would be the same way. I can see where he would expect me to just believe his promises and let him back in. That was not in my mind at all.

He hadn't really met the new Michelle yet. I tried to introduce myself in our letters, but his letters were so overwhelming that I didn't write that often. Sometimes he asked me to write more frequently, but how could I? I was overwhelmed. Overwhelmed with responsibility I now held all on my own and overwhelmed by the feelings that John's letters evoked in me.

My nights were restless and my days full. Still, life was much better than I'd seen in Boston. It was stable and I was in charge. I was no longer at the beck and call of a drug addict. I was no longer living in the eye of the storm.

Some of John's letters were short and others were long. Some felt more like diaries than letters. It seemed like he was busy at Teen Challenge. In one of his letters, he described his days.

*February 1990*

*Hi, Michelle.*

*How is the new house? It sounds nice from what you told me over the phone. Having a two-car garage with electric doors is real nice on snowy days. I wish I were there to enjoy it too. Well, someday.*

*Where are the letters you were going to send? Did you forget to write? They usually pass the mail out around 6:00pm, but tonight we had a youth group here so the mail is late. Well, they walked into my room with two letters and a card. I'll pick up where I left off in the morning. I want to read your letters and get to bed. I love you. Good night.*

*I read your letters and they made me so happy. Please send me pictures of the house and of you; plus the boys' pictures.*

*Listen, those things I wrote about in the letters, please forget them. I love you so much; it hurts being without you.*

*Saturday, we have a big breakfast schedule. First we have a public devotion as a group and then breakfast at 10:30am. Then, we have free time until 5:00pm. Monday we work all day. Tuesday through Friday, we go to the Learning Center to learn the Bible from 8:00am until 11:30am. Then, lunch at 12:00pm. We work around here from 1:00pm to 4:30pm. Hopefully, I'll get to work at the garage every day. I feel at home there. Well, not exactly home, but close to home.*

*I was looking at the picture of you on our honeymoon. You are wearing your yellow sundress. You look so beautiful! You are a gift from God. I tell everyone that.*

*How are you tonight? It's Saturday night and it's all right. Well, it's so-so without you. I finished helping a friend of mine here write a letter to his wife. They have been separated for five years.*

*I can't wait to see you on March 3. I hope you plan on coming. I'd love you to bring my Bible and the Bible on cassette. I can't wait for you to send me my wedding ring.*

*I wish you could see me now. I have put on so much weight. I weigh 175 pounds. Can you believe it? My roommate told me I'm looking younger every day. He said I have a "glow." God is restoring me.*

*Happy Valentine's Day. I feel better when I'm writing you. I have already written too much. You probably won't have time to read all three pages. Well, I'm going to bed, it is almost 10:30pm now. I love you, Michelle and I'll write a little more tomorrow, okay? Good night, I love you!*

A few days later, his toned changed. I got a letter where he was almost belligerent to me. He was angry because I hadn't written in a few days and hadn't sent him pictures. He called me out for having my own interests now. He told me not to worry about it as he had stopped thinking and caring for me too. He told me to hold on to my letters and my pictures because he didn't want them.

He went on to tell me that he'd received a restriction from the staff that day. He'd called someone a name and lost his phone privilege for the week. He made it worse by reacting negatively to the punishment and they gave him 15 more hours of restriction. He said he wasn't doing well but assured me that if he did leave Teen Challenge, he wouldn't be coming to New York.

That was John's pattern. He was great at playing the victim. This time, however, I wasn't going to play the enabler. I waited a few days before I responded so that I didn't erupt all over the paper as I might have in the past. Instead I kept it cool and sent it along with a few clothing items that he'd previously requested.

Sure enough, his tone flip-flopped once he received the package, and his letters were filled with words of love again. I don't know how many times I cried reading his letters. I realized that if he and I would ever have a chance of reconciling, I was going to have to do some more work on myself. I was going to have to learn how to have a healthy relationship with my husband and not be drawn into the old patterns just as much as he was trying to break them himself. I realized I had been as sick as he was for a very long time.

If I was going to let him back into my life on any level, I was going to have to learn to react differently to his mood swings. I couldn't let them continue to impact me.

I craved normalcy in my life. On the day that Daniel, our youngest, turned 5, I was praying that I wouldn't receive a letter from John. I wanted to be bright for our son and his friends. I'd planned a small party for him.

Sure enough, I didn't get a letter from John, but worse. The phone rang. One of my assistants at the daycare answered the phone and told me that the director of Teen Challenge was on the other end of the line. I knew it couldn't be good news. My heart was pounding in my chest.

I really wasn't ready for what he had to say, "Hi, Michelle. It's Jimmy V. I was wondering if John was there with you?" Could I have heard that right?! Jimmy V. went on to tell me that John had packed his things and left the program. They suspected that he might turn up at my house in New York. Hearing that, I collapsed into a nearby chair. How could this be possible?

I hadn't told John our address and Jimmy V. swore that he hadn't either. Jimmy V. said that he'd give John until 6:00pm to return to the program or he'd be notifying the police of his departure.

It wasn't too long after that when I got a second call, this time from my brother. Apparently, John had called him asking for my phone number. Thankfully, Joe didn't give it to him but instead got John's number at a pay phone so I could call him back. My brother told me that he was trying to get on a bus to Albany. Knowing him, John was trying to get here for Daniel's birthday. I needed to call him right away.

I called John and asked him what he was thinking, leaving Teen Challenge when the courts didn't allow him to legally do so. I didn't really give him an opportunity to answer before I asked him if he'd rather see divorce papers or a completion certificate from Teen Challenge? I told him that he had to be back at Teen Challenge before 6:00pm or he'd be expelled from the program and sent back to jail. Is that what he wanted?

I told him emphatically that there was no opportunity for him to come to New York to my house. If he did not go back to the center, to Teen Challenge, and he showed up here, I let him know that I would call the police and have him arrested.

John tried to explain that he wanted to come see the kids and me, but I wasn't listening. Why couldn't he see the bigger picture instead of just focusing on his immediate desires? My brother must have jumped in the car as soon as we ended our call because he walked into my kitchen just as I was about to really lose it with John. He saw the look on my face and told me to take a deep breath.

He went upstairs and picked up the other extension. He told John to stop and think about what he was doing. He encouraged him to go back to the program and finish the program. It was the only way that John would see his boys again.

While we were talking with John, the director called me back. I gave Jimmy V. the number to the pay phone. I said goodbye to John and hung up. I knew that Jimmy V. was going to call him next. Thinking it was me, John picked the receiver up and was quite shocked to hear Jimmy V.'s voice. He knew he was in trouble.

Meanwhile, back in New York, I was a mess. I ran up into the bathroom and collapsed on the floor. This was much worse than one of his letters. I knew that he wanted to be in New York with us, but why couldn't he see the damage he was doing to us?

I knew I had to pull myself together for my son. It wasn't his fault that his father was a broken man. It wasn't his fault that his mother was a hot mess. Thankfully, he was having fun with his friends and his brothers, unaware of what was happening behind the scenes.

When I went back downstairs, the kids in my daycare were just waking up from their naps. I was thankful to have my assistants help with the kids and my brother to lean on for emotional support. I still didn't know if John would make his way back to Teen Challenge before 6:00pm or if he'd show up at my door. I couldn't imagine calling the police on him, right in front of the boys.

We celebrated Daniel's birthday that afternoon. It was probably a good thing his party was that day. It was a little bit of a distraction. On the outside, everything looked normal. On the inside, my stomach was in knots.

At 6:05pm, Jim called me and let me know that John had returned to the program. He'd dragged it out until the very last moment, but the good news was that he'd returned. I felt such a relief. I felt like I could finally breathe again.

Maybe John did have a shot at making it. He had listened to reason and walked away from the brief taste of freedom he'd experienced. His behavior was changing for the better because the old John would never have gone back to Teen Challenge. Had John really let God back into his life? Even though it had been a rough day, I actually felt a little bit encouraged when I laid down to sleep that night. Daniel and his brothers had so much fun that day. I was thankful that they were oblivious to the drama that had transpired.

# 11
## Chapter

*Getting to know Christ*

John returned to the Teen Challenge program, but the highs and lows followed him there. It felt like there were a lot more lows than there were highs. It must have been difficult for him, having lived the high life where he was the owner of a large, successful garage to now working for someone else for free. He'd lost any privileges that he'd previously accrued and now he was starting over. The restrictions were indefinite. I remember Jimmy V. telling me that we were going to see what John was really made of. These restrictions were either going to make him or break him. Again, his rebellious nature had gotten him into trouble and John was having to learn his lessons the hard way, but maybe this time they would stick. I was encouraged by Jimmy V. sharing with me that these ups and downs were normal during recovery. This was why the Teen Challenge program was longer than the shorter programs that John had tried in the past. This program accounted for the back and forth, up and down that happens during recovery, giving students the chance to become better adjusted to life without drugs or alcohol.

As for me, I kept moving forward. Without a doubt, John's returning to the program gave me the hope that I needed. On the outside, it might have seemed very insignificant, but to me the return spoke volumes. Instead of running when his life got tougher, John was finding the strength to stand his ground. In turn, this was giving me the strength that I needed, or at least adding to the strength that I so desperately needed to get through it all on my own.

I was changing too. Having found my own voice, I wasn't going to squelch it any more. I wasn't letting John walk all over me any more, even if it was just in letters since he wouldn't be able to call me until he earned that privilege again. I was speaking up, clearly stating what was on my own mind, and I wasn't giving into easily agreeing to whatever ideas he was throwing out there, no matter how convincingly he was pleading his case.

I didn't know it at the time, but now when I look back I can see that I was beginning to construct healthier boundaries in my life. I was learning to stand up for myself. I was getting to know what I was good at and what I wasn't good at. I was also stepping into a world that allowed me to do things that I enjoyed, just because I enjoyed them. I didn't have to justify any of my actions to anyone. These first months in New York were a time of significant personal growth for me. I grew to know myself better at the same time that I was getting to know Christ better.

The letters kept coming and in them John incessantly referred to the day when he'd come home to be with the boys and me. His words made my stomach lurch each time I read them. Of course, I was nervous about accepting that kind of disturbance, for lack of a better description, into my life again, but even more so, I was put off by the assumptions that he was making. I know that we committed to 'until death do us part,' but I really felt that I was owed the opportunity to voice my thoughts on this matter. As far as I was concerned, at this point all bets were off.

I had already told John on several occasions that he would not be welcome home if he didn't complete the Teen Challenge program, but in my mind that didn't directly translate to arms open wide if or when he did graduate from the program. It was something that we would have to discuss – a lot, in the future. I would have to do a lot of praying on this.

Because it might throw him off track, I kept my mouth shut and pen away from writing about these feelings for the time being. No sense sending him into a tailspin when he was finally working hard to get better. Still, I kept formulating my responses to those comments, again and again. I would undoubtedly be ready to discuss the transition when the time came, even if John wasn't.

The real anxiety driver was our upcoming trip to Boston. Half-expecting the visit to be rescheduled because of John's sometimes rebellious behavior, when the time came the boys and I were ready. My brother Joe made the trek with us and he brought along a friend.

This would be the first time the boys had a chance to sit and talk with John in months. It was the first time they'd have an opportunity to talk with a sober John in what was probably many months. We talked about the fact that John might mention coming to Albany and living with us at some point. I really didn't want them to get their hopes up and felt it best to counter those comments up front. There was no reason in having them get their hopes up only to have John dash them with his rebellious, rash behavior. I planned to pull John aside when we got there and ask him not to bring up that subject in front of the boys.

The boys told me they understood what I was trying to tell them and it seemed like they did understand to the extent that their young minds allowed. I knew they would still be nervous about seeing John. Heck, I was an adult and I was nervous. I kept taking deep breaths and prayed silently on the long drive over. My brother's friend also helped to distract me from the anxious thoughts floating through my mind.

Then the moment arrived. We pulled into the Teen Challenge parking lot and it was time to go meet my estranged husband. I felt like I was moving in slow motion, even though my heart was beating out of control in my chest. Somehow, I kept my voice level and encouraged the boys to go on ahead. In my mind, it would be easier if the boys broke the ice for us.

When it was my turn to greet John, we shared a very stiff hug, but not totally unpleasant hug. It felt more like a hug I might give a stranger rather than my husband of 10 years. When I stepped back, I had to admit that John was looking much healthier than the last time I'd seen him. My heart might have reacted to the sight of him, but my head knew it was the changes on the inside that were most important.

Without being sure of the ground on which we stood, I was more quiet than normal. I just didn't trust the man that I married any more. He'd broken my heart one too many times. The good news is that he was more than excited to see the boys and catch up with them. A few times

I joined the conversation when it turned to the subject of our new home and the life we were building in New York, but even then, I wasn't able to rouse much emotion. There was a numbness inside of me and more than anything, I was looking forward to when this visit would end and I could be on my way again.

Even though John's stay was restricted, he was not supervised 24x7. Our visit wasn't governed by strict rules. We took a tour of the facility and the boys even enjoyed birthday cake with one of the other residents. After a while, they became restless and I gave them permission to play a bit. At the same time, my brother and his friend stepped outside and explored the grounds. This left John and I face to face.

His eyes looked so sincere to me, but I couldn't help being leery of the words coming out of his mouth. He'd always been able to sweet talk me and I needed to guard myself from falling into old patterns. Thankfully, the conversation remained benign and for the first time in longer than I could remember, we didn't end up screaming and yelling at one another. Instead, it felt like a normal adult conversation. I wasn't ready to trust this new relationship we were forging, not in any way shape or form, but I could at least acknowledge that it felt different, in a good way.

When we did finally leave and I climbed into the car, I still didn't allow myself to let out the emotions that I'd been bottling up inside of me during the visit. I didn't want to upset the boys who were so happy to have spent time with their father. It was difficult to see John living this life. Sure, it was leaps and bounds better than prison, but he was still unable to lead a free life. At the same time, I was happy about the atmosphere there. It was totally different than what I'd been used to with the secular 30 day programs that John had previously attended. The boys played basketball with some of the other students; we had a nice dinner and overall, it was very uplifting. So many conflicting emotions ran through me. I was sad to see him there, but I was also relieved to see him there. I wanted to hug him, but I also wanted to run away from him. I wanted to lean on him and I wanted to push him away. I knew that I was going to have to pray long and hard, letting the comfort and grace of the Holy Spirit wash over me. I needed God's guidance to see me through.

# 12
## Chapter

## Getting Reacquainted

Back home in New York, I continued to dodge questions about John. When anyone asked, I explained in a tone that let everyone know the topic wasn't up for discussion, that we were recently separated and that he was living in another state. There was enough inner turmoil and judgment; I didn't need to listen to anyone else's thoughts on the matter. Once in a while I leaned on the few close friendships I'd developed, but for the most part, no one knew that John was residing in a drug and alcohol rehabilitation center in Boston and I preferred it that way.

Jimmy V. continued to call me and the reports on John's behavior kept improving. He had other visitors now. Our church friends in Boston made it a point to stop by and see him. They'd also reach out to me and let me know how they thought he was doing. Things seemed to be progressing in the right direction.

Before we knew it, summer was upon us and the boys were out of school. We'd fallen into a kind of routine where we'd visit John monthly, but with the additional free time of summer, we decided to visit John more frequently. It helped that John was adhering to the program's strict rules and was afforded semi-monthly visits.

The boys enjoyed seeing their father more often and, if I was being honest, I was beginning to enjoy our visits too. It was becoming easier for me to see the positive changes in John. He seemed happier than I'd seen him in years, happier on the inside. At the same time, I couldn't let go of the fears that held me back. Even though I could see positive changes in John, I wasn't ready to trust him. Instead, I just enjoyed the time we spent together. I kept it real by living in the moment and I thought and talked less about the future. Maybe I was running from it. Whatever the reason, I was focused on the day-to-day stuff, sharing my life's stories with John and listening to what was going on in his days.

On some level, we were getting reacquainted. We were reconnecting. We'd both changed a lot from the people that we were when we first met. I wanted to think that we'd both grown stronger and more clear. We'd both welcomed Jesus Christ into our lives. We both wanted the same things out of life, but only time would tell if we'd make our dreams come true together or not.

About six months into the program, I was standing in my kitchen facing the backyard when I felt an urgency to call the Teen Challenge center. We exchanged letters, visited regularly, but it was very unusual for me to pick up the phone and call. Just the same, I called about him that day. I had to. I sensed something was wrong with my husband.

When the director answered the phone, he was shocked to hear my voice. He quickly updated me on the current situation. John was in his room hurriedly packing his bags. He'd decided that he was leaving the program again. Jimmy V. was disappointed, but he wasn't going to try to stop him. Whether he stayed or left had to be up to John.

I asked to speak with John but wasn't allowed to. Jimmy V. didn't want me to influence John either. If he was going to stay, he had to make the decision himself. That was the only way it was going to work. Jimmy V. assured me that he'd let me know what the outcome was and I reluctantly hung up the phone.

Hearing what was going on in Boston brought up old emotions. Distrust, anger, fear, they all came jumping out of the woodwork to assault my senses. I did my best to turn my focus toward the Holy Spirit. I prayed that God would help John in ways that I couldn't.

Hours passed and Jimmy V. eventually called with an update. Apparently, John had gotten angry at a worker and threatened to leave the program again. Another resident of the program was also upset and helped to fuel John's fire. Somehow, I'm sure by the grace of God, John found reason and stayed put even when his friend exited the program. Just the same, John lost all of his privileges again.

Because of John's actions, the boys and I were no longer allowed to visit every other week and there were no more phone calls. It was back to solely relying on letters to communicate with one another. That made it harder on the boys and I hated to tell them about the change. Once again, I was having to deal with the fallout of John's actions. When we wrapped up our call, the director shared that we'd again get to see what John was made of. Dealing with indefinite restrictions would make or break my husband.

On a positive note, as time went on, despite renewed restrictions governing his actions, John seemed to be growing more settled in the program. His rebellious behavior was rarely seen and he'd begun asking for greater responsibility. In addition to working in the garage, John became responsible for keeping the wood stoves stocked and burning during the colder months. John willingly tended to the stoves while others were sleeping soundly in their beds and he never complained about it. In his reports to me, the director was pleased by John's actions and demeanor.

That winter, John was once again able to receive visitors and the boys and I headed to Boston. I couldn't believe how much I wanted to see him this time. It felt much different than our first visit to Teen Challenge, even though that was just 8 months before. It still amazes me how much my feelings changed in that short period of time. Similar to how John experienced ups and downs, I did too. Staying focused on the present and leaning on the Holy Spirit allowed me to move through it and find a calmer place from which to live. I was still unsure of how it was all going to work out, but I was beginning to entertain the idea that maybe John would one day join us in New York, and we could live like a family again.

Because John still had restrictions levied against him, our hopes of an overnight visit for our wedding anniversary were dashed. Again, I was surprised at how disappointed I felt over that. I know it would have been an emotional rollercoaster and I wasn't sure what it'd be like to be in

John's company for more than a couple of hours, but I was at the point where I was willing to try. Unfortunately, I'd have to wait a little longer for that experiment to happen.

On the day of our anniversary, I received a letter from Pastor Bossio. We hadn't spoken since the conference in Washington, DC, two years prior, but I was quickly reminded of the insightful words he'd shared with me. He'd told me then that I would walk through deep waters and without a doubt, I had. I was really hoping that only shallow waters were ahead of me now.

Apparently, Pastor Gay had shared my address with Pastor Bossio and I was very encouraged by what I read. In truth, I was standing at the mailbox, jumping up and down. Once again, God used Pastor Bossio to lift me up during my difficult time. I knew the Holy Spirit had to be leading him because I hadn't spoken with Pastor Bossio in so long.

I leaned back in my chair, took a deep breath and exhaled very slowly. I was trying to let his words sink in. It felt like a lifetime had passed since I'd met Pastor Bossio at that conference. He was right on about me walking through deep waters and I hoped that he was right about God restoring John.

In the letter, Pastor Bossio included reference to a passage in the Bible and I was moved to read it promptly. Psalm 37:23-28 reads, "If the Lord delights in a man's way, He makes his steps firm; though he may stumble, he'll not fall, for the Lord upholds him with His hand. I was young and now I'm old, yet I have never seen the righteous forsaken or their children begging bread. They are generous and lend freely; their children will be blessed. Turn from evil, do good; then you will dwell in the land forever. For the Lord loves them and will not forsake His faithful ones. They will be protected forever, but the offspring of the wicked will be cut off."

These words were very comforting. Although John and I had stumbled through the years, God was there to catch us. As long as we believed and did our best to uphold His teachings, God would bless us.

It was the encouragement that I needed on this day when I'd found myself blue and battling feelings of disappointment. With his words, Pastor Bossio helped me to see the Light of God on my path again. I knew that I was ready to more firmly commit myself to serving as a vessel of God. I didn't know exactly what God had in mind, but I was there for

Him. I was also relieved to know that God was committed to helping John because I knew that I wasn't capable of holding him up myself.

It amazed me then and still amazes me today, the ways in which God works. At just the right time, He reached out to me in a way that I could understand and let me know that everything was going to be ok. I was reassured that I was still on the right path and that even though I didn't have all the answers, I didn't need to. God had everything under control. While I might not be able to trust John, I knew that I could trust God. What a special gift I'd been given on that special day.

God continued to work in mysterious ways and I did my best to be open and receptive to what He asked of me. In September that year, John sent me a letter telling me about what he believed to be an exceptionally exciting opportunity. The Teen Challenge choir routinely sang at Christian Churches, even when they had to travel in order to do so. John did not sing in the choir, so I wasn't at first sure why he would bring this up to me. Setting my confusion aside, I continued to read and saw that the leaders at Teen Challenge had given John permission to travel with the choir based on his outstanding behavior during his recent restrictive period.

When he got right down to it, John asked me to talk to Pastor Gay about inviting the choir to sing right there at our church - right down the street from my house, not only the choir, but John. He gave me the ins and outs of it, asking for three services to sing at in one weekend.

My head just about exploded when I read John's request. Sure, he was excited about the opportunity, but I hadn't even gotten my head around his coming to Albany when he completed the program, let alone at the half-way point.

Did I want to let my unpredictable husband know where the boys and I lived? I'd worked so hard to keep that information from him. I never wanted him to just show up on my doorstep. If truth be told, I didn't want him breaking into my house again and stealing from me. He had a habit of not only stealing material things, he also stole my sense of security.

How could he ask that of me? To make myself vulnerable again? I was just starting to get my legs under me. Finally in a place where I didn't have to worry about John interrupting the boys' and my stability, I decided not to respond right away. Without a doubt, prayer was needed.

Pray I did and it was through prayer that I could see that I could open my house to John without giving my power back to him. Healthier myself, I could exercise my rights, my control over the situation. I decided that I would help the choir come to Albany to sing, but that it wouldn't be for another month or so.

Surprisingly, it felt good to make a decision that involved John in my life. The difference this time was that it was actually a healthy decision. I was nervous about opening up to John in this way, but I was also excited about it. So were the boys.

When we visited on Saturdays, we were allowed to stay in an apartment on the Teen Challenge campus and the boys were thrilled with that arrangement. I knew that having their dad 'home' again, even briefly, really gave them hope that someday our family life would return to normal.

That thought made me chuckle to myself. What was normal anyway? There was no way we were going back to the old normal. We still needed to define a new normal. Perhaps a visit from John would help to clarify that in my mind. It might help me to visualize what a home life might be like with a sober John, a John who was interested in conversation and spending time with his wife and children, a John who didn't spend weekends out with the boys.

It wasn't long before the weekend arrived for the choir to visit Albany. We had worked it out that John would stay at the house with the boys and me. The assistant director and his wife, as well as a couple of choir members, also stayed with us. Having the extra people there took some of the pressure off of me and I didn't feel as awkward having John at the house as I feared I might.

That afternoon, the two young men that were also staying at the house sat at the kitchen table and conversed. I was busy getting things ready for dinner but couldn't help but overhear the conversation between the two young men. It wasn't the content that drew my attention but the severe stuttering that plagued one of them. I was immediately compelled to pray for this young man but faltered when I realized I hadn't yet learned his name.

Setting aside my dinner preparations, I turned to this young man and asked his name. When he told me he was called "David," I asked if he minded if I prayed for him. He gave me a beautiful smile and graciously accepted my offer.

Feeling more than a little awkward, this wasn't something I routinely did with strangers; I walked over to the table and placed my hands on David's shoulders. I prayed for this young man and felt the peace and calm come over me that the Holy Spirit always brings me in prayer. Now, with a smile on my face too, I felt that I'd done what I was supposed to do and the strong urge was released.

Heading back to the counter and planning to finish getting dinner ready, I noticed that David had stood up from the table. He thanked me for the meaningful prayer and it was then that we both realized his words came out of his mouth clearly and smoothly. He'd lost his stutter! I later found out that while he'd previously been blessed with the gift of song, he'd never been able to enjoy unrehearsed conversation without struggling through his words.

I ran upstairs to get the assistant director and then I called Pastor Gay and asked him to come over. John and the Teen Challenge staff were also just getting back from a quick trip to the store. Everyone listened to David speak excitedly, quickly, and confidently for the first time in his life.

Everyone was quiet while the realization of what was happening started to sink in. No one knew what to say. I did. I had witnessed a miracle in my own kitchen. The Holy Spirit worked a wonder with this young man, blessed him and gave him his voice.

I forgot about all the worries I'd had leading up to this weekend. The joy of witnessing a miracle and, if there was a way for it to be even more special, being able to share it with not only Pastor Gay but with John too made it incredibly special for me.

# 13
## Chapter

## Releasing the Past

Two weeks later, I went to Boston alone. John and I really needed to have time to talk just amongst ourselves. Fifteen minutes a week on the phone just wasn't enough. On the days preceding the visit, I had a sense that something was wrong. I prayed and even fasted for 3 days before I headed east. That wasn't anything I'd ever done before, but I felt like this needed my attention. I needed to be clear if I was going to hear what the Spirit of God was trying to tell me.

It was becoming clear that, in order to move forward, I was going to have to release my past. Forgiving John was going to be a big step for me and not one I was sure that I could take on my own. The Holy Spirit was making it clear to me, however, that accepting what pain I had endured as a result of my past relationship with John was the only way that we could build a future together.

Feeling unsure and more vulnerable than I'd felt in months, there was no denying that it was God's intention that I meet with my husband alone. When I arrived at Teen Challenge, I was greeted by Jimmy V. and John. There was an uncomfortable silence and I didn't know why. I immediately looked at John and asked him what was wrong. John remained silent, but Jimmy V. explained that he'd been counseling John on something important. Still, nothing from John.

To fill the space, I mentioned that I'd been praying all week, feeling the heaviness in the air and Jimmy V. confessed that he'd been praying for us too. He then suggested that we take a few hours off-campus to spend time together as a couple and both John and I agreed that was a good idea.

In the car, there was a heaviness again. We found a quiet place where we could sit and talk. For the first time in a long time, John and I were alone, really alone. We were able to talk from the heart. John told me about all the guilt he was carrying around, knowing the pain that he'd caused me. He told me of his transgressions, some of which I'd already been aware and others that were new to me. I tried to take it all in, but it was a lot for me to digest. John asked me to forgive him and let us start over with a clean slate. I knew that was what the Holy Spirit had been preparing me for all week, but letting go of the pain and opening myself up for more was still just beyond my reach. I could accept what he told me about the past, but I was afraid to accept the new scenario he laid out in front of me.

More serious than I'd ever seen him before, I struggled to trust his newly found sincerity. I'd heard the words many times in the past, but was he really being honest this time? In my heart of hearts, I realized that I felt safe for the first time in a very long time. Maybe I really could move on from the past.

John searched my face for an answer. I sat up a little straighter and looked him in the eye. "John, I accept what has gone before us and I forgive you. We have to let the past go and embrace a future which God has prepared for us." I think he could read the sincerity in my voice because I saw the muscles in his face relax. We prayed together and asked God to protect our new life together. We cried and we hugged. I felt like a messenger with love pouring out of me and onto John. It was clear that the weight of knowing the pain he'd caused had been lifted from his shoulders and before we left our quiet place, there was once again a sparkle in his eye.

I was reminded of Corinthians 13:4-8a, "Love is patient. Love is kind. It doesn't envy. It does not boast. It is not proud. It is not rude. It is not self-seeking. It is not easily angered and it keeps no records of wrongs. Love does not delight in evil, but rejoices with the truth. It always protects, always trusts, always hopes, and always perseveres. Love never fails."

It was the act of forgiveness that allowed us to start over. Our relationship began to grow again now that there was no more guilt snuffing the life out of it. We still had to face John's addiction and the work that he would continue to do in order to master that, but together we were strong. Entrusting God to watch over us and help John with his addiction was a key part of this new relationship we were building together. We both knew that in order to have the life together that we longed for, we'd need to trust in God to help us find our way.

Our four hours off-campus went by quickly. John's hand found mine on the way back in the car and I felt the connection spread between us. I had a lot to think about on the drive home that day, but I knew we were headed in the right direction.

John told me later that Jimmy V. was surprised at how well I reacted to his confession. I had been angry at him for many years, always suspicious and repelled by his lies and reckless lifestyle. The week before our visit, God spoke to me in a way that I could understand. His message told me it was time to let the anger and the suspicions go. It was time to move on. When I saw John and he confessed to things that I'd spent time worrying about, I knew it was God's confirmation that our past was behind us. John was finally owning the mistakes that he had made and was asking forgiveness. It was up to me to grant this forgiveness and, knowing God was behind me, supporting me, I was strong enough to do it. I no longer harbored any anger toward John. I'd given enough energy to that in the past. My present focus was on building a strong future with my husband and my sons. A future like I'd never before imagined.

When I look back at this time, I too am surprised by a lack of reaction, but in hindsight, I can see that a heavy weight had been lifted from my shoulders too.

A few days later, in the middle of the afternoon I needed to run a quick errand. I left the children in the care of my assistants and jumped in the car. Before I made it to the store, an old song came on the radio that reminded me of John's and my time together. I felt the emotions come up that had passed through me so quickly on our Saturday visit.

The tears came flooding down my face and I turned the car around. There was no way that I could run to the store in the state that I was in.

The phone was ringing as I walked through the door. My assistant yelled up to me that Jimmy V. and John were on the phone. When I was calmed down enough to answer, Jimmy V. expressed concern over me. He said that he sensed I wasn't myself when I left Saturday and they just wanted to call and check on me. I did my best to hold back the sobs, but they came through anyway. He probably didn't believe me when I tried to assure him I was fine. He put John on the phone and my husband prayed for me. I told him not to worry about me, but I really didn't have anything else to say. I was still trying to get my own head around what was happening to me.

Exhausted by all the emotions, I went to bed early that night. I was fighting inner demons, ones that I had been sure I'd already defeated. I called on the Holy Spirit to help me walk through this valley of death. I had to kill these demons, releasing them so that I could once again embrace love and life. I knew I couldn't do it on my own. I needed help letting go of the pain and the anger it caused within me. I was tired and I needed to lean on God.

With my arms outstretched, I committed to handing over my negative emotions to God. While I'd like to say it was easy, it wasn't. I had to do this over and over again until I could truly release the pain that had welled up inside of me. Never for a moment did I doubt that God was willing to accept my pain, but pain and fear had been my companion for many years. I knew pain and was used to having pain in my life. I'd forgotten what life could be like without it.

I knew from my Bible studies that if we don't forgive, we won't be forgiven and we will be judged in the same way. Whenever these emotions came up for me, I leaned on God. Over time, I was able to fully forgive John. Forgetting was another hurdle and that took years, but I knew that John and our marriage were worth saving. I did not want my boys to be without their father. In my heart, I loved John and I knew that he loved me too. With our combined love and our trust in God to help us, we could be more than survivors of our past; we would be the creators of a strong, loving future for our family.

During the next few months, John and I began to talk more about the day that he would be released from Teen Challenge. I spent that time preparing in my mind for his coming to Albany to be near the boys and me. That was a lot to prepare for. I knew that there was no way I was going backward. Never again would I live in fear. With my trust in God, I looked forward to a life filled with peace and calm.

Then, just like that, John's fifteen months at Teen Challenge were over. Even though we'd seen him on Saturday, it was a surprise when Monday morning I got a call from Jimmy V. telling me that John's stay was over. Just like that. No formal actions signifying the great accomplishment or to help prepare me for what was to come next.

A short while later, I got a call from John himself. He had caught a bus and was on his way to Albany. I didn't know what time to expect him, but he was on his way. I called my girlfriend to come sit with me and her husband went to wait at the bus station for John. My nerves were rattled.

This wasn't at all how I had envisioned his home coming. My friend's husband went to the train station several times that day, looking for John. We had no inkling as to when he'd arrive, but at 5pm that afternoon he knocked on my front door with a suitcase in his hand. He found his way to my house all on his own. I invited John in and let Jimmy V. know he'd arrived safely.

To be honest, I wasn't really ready for John to move back in. I thought he'd spend time transitioning first, but that's not how it worked out. While it was a relief to have the 'sentence' fulfilled and the program completed, I wasn't yet ready to trust his ability to master his addiction going forward.

Ready or not, here he was. While he played with the boys, I called Pastor Gay and that helped to quell my fears a bit. As much as we'd talked leading up to this, John and I had not talked about his moving in with me right away. I'd pretty much averted the conversation whenever John tried to bring it up. Obviously, that wasn't my smartest idea.

My parents had coached me not to take him back into my life and my home, but here he was. I felt like I was walking on eggshells now that he was here and I'm sure that my work suffered a bit while I got used to the idea of it.

My first priority was taking care of our sons and protecting them from any hurt and disappointment like they had already experienced in the past with their father. I found it very difficult to let John integrate fully into the family as father and husband again. I didn't trust him and was almost waiting for him to hurt us again. In my heart I wanted us to be together and a happy family, but the trust was just not there. He hadn't proved himself to me yet.

The boys and I finally had stability in our lives and I didn't want to jeopardize that. I tried to control everything. Every time John went out the door to look for a job, I'd hold my breath until he got back. If he was out and the phone rang, I'd panic for a moment, dreading bad news. The past was always there and I was always reacting to those reminders of what had happened and what could happen.

My distrust of John led to many disagreements and a great deal of tension between us. I was trying hard to hide our issues from the boys, but I was in a constant state of emotional upheaval. I know now that I was being hypervigilant. I probably had a little Post Traumatic Stress Disorder from all of the events that had transpired.

Eventually, I was able to turn my fears and doubts over to God. To do that, my head was in the Bible constantly. I read my favorite passages over and over again, which gave me great comfort. There were days I'd just lay down and pray, imploring God to help me get through it.

I was very torn between my boys, my parents and my brothers; afraid they would feel slighted and resentful because I'd once again allowed John to come back into our lives. I really wasn't putting him first, not ahead of our children, but I was afraid it might look that way to others. I knew that if our home ever became unsafe, I would always protect my boys from hurt. My goal was just to have my family back together again. I really didn't want my kids to come from a broken family.

Looking back, I can see where my extended family might have felt like I was putting John first. I gave him so much of my attention because I felt I needed to in order to make sure everything was as it needed to be. If I could prevent him from tearing apart our family with reckless behavior, I thought everything would be fine. I didn't realize that in doing so, I was taking some of my attention away from my children. Although they were well taken care of, I regret to this day that many times my mind was focused on survival and how to keep the family together. It was seldom that I felt comfortable just kicking back and playing with the kids.

Spending time playing with my grandsons really points this out to me now.

When I look back at how I was then, I realize that I had become a different person. I was living in a state of fight or flight. I was filled with constant anxiety just getting through the day. I worried about paying the bills, keeping the roof over our heads, food on the table; tuition paid, etc. On top of that, I worried that my husband would slip up and destroy the fragile home that we'd built in New York. John was supposed to be the head of the family. My father was the head of my family growing up. I felt like I had to do whatever it took to mold my family into the same structure that I grew up in.

I had a certain vision in my mind, but the man I married must have had an entirely different picture in his mind. I was used to having my father come home for dinner at 5pm and we'd all talk about our days. In my adult life, I'd put the roast in the oven, but so many times John never came home to dinner. That was the case in so many areas of our life together. No matter how hard I tried to emulate my childhood for my own kids, it just didn't happen.

While I'd grown up with a faith in God, I'd only seen the Bible as something to dust every now and again. It was through the rocky path my marriage brought me that I learned the Bible was more than just a book of old stories. It was through this difficult journey that my faith began to grow into something greater than just a teaching in my head. My faith had blossomed in my heart as a knowing that those old words were applicable to my life each and every day.

Thankfully, my faith overrode any of the fears that I was battling about the family we were becoming. By putting my faith into practice, I was able to see a more stable future for us. For the first time in a very long time, I did have trust. It was trust in God and His love for not only me, but for my family too. Proverbs 3:5 came to mind again, "Trust in the Lord with all your heart and lean not on your own understanding. In all your ways, acknowledge Him and He will direct your path."

Thank goodness, too, for the friendships I had built. Their support gave me a sense of normalcy in my life. With John beside me again, we began to get reacquainted. He really did seem to have changed. Because of the changes he'd made, he was kind of a stranger to me and I prayed that I would love the new man that he'd become.

Our transition wasn't as smooth as it might have been. I wish we'd gotten some counseling to prepare us. After just two weeks of his being in New York, my parents came for a visit. They stayed in Clifton Park at my brothers' and I was grateful for even that short distance between us. It would be the first time they'd seen him in almost two years. Just thinking about that made my insides tremble.

Pastor Gay and his wife Joyce came over to help smooth out any rough edges during their visit. There were many uncomfortable silences, but it had to be clear to them that the boys were excited to have their father home and we somehow survived the visit without bruises.

Shortly thereafter, my brother's temporary job agency placed John at a local garage where he was hired immediately. Although I was glad to see John productive in our community and being a breadwinner again, it became a daily worry for me. I worried that he might fall back into old habits once he was working in a garage where it wasn't unusual to go drinking with your coworkers at the end of the day.

A few months later, a neighbor told us about an opening at a nationwide auto center down the road. He applied for the service advisor role and with his wealth of experience, was quickly hired. John was always a hard worker and that hadn't changed.

I could tell that John wanted to be the man of the house, the one taking care of all our financial needs again. I had changed too and become more self-sufficient than the wife he had remembered. This was something else that we both had to adjust to. John was showing me a lot of patience and I was doing my best to let him back into my life. Every day I had to remind myself to share with him what had, in his absence, become my total responsibility. Every day was a battle in my mind to let go of the reins and trust him to do what I thought was the right thing for our family.

There was no question that having someone to share the workload with was a relief. I didn't realize how exhausting it had been to take care of things all on my own. While one part of me fought against the desire to lean in, the other part of me welcomed the extra help John provided.

Pastor Gay did step in and counsel us on all of the changes that were thrust upon us. We worked on trust, respect, parenting, coupling, and even the need for each of us to have some alone time. John started attending Trinity Christian Church with the boys and me and he was quickly welcomed by the congregation. He was quickly accepted into our community by my friends. Everyone I knew had been praying for us this past year and they all were pleased to see what they were sure was a success story. I wished I'd felt as confident of our success as my friends did.

Life seemed to be moving forward and I needed to keep up the pace. The boys seemed to be adjusting to the new dynamics in our home and I needed to as well. At night, the boys were busy with their sporting practices and on the weekends John and I enjoyed their games.

During the week, I continued working with the daycare are and John went off to the garage. There was a part of me that worried when he took this new job at the autocenter. I was afraid that he'd find new friends who shared an old habit. While I had forgiven him, it was hard to let go of those worries. This was all still so new for me. Each day when he came home from work, I silently let out a sigh of relief.

Negative thoughts continued to plague my mind and it was wearing me out. Talking to Pastor Gay did help, but the work of trusting John was exhausting. While his behaviors and actions were consistent, I just couldn't let it go. I had vowed to myself that I would never go backward. If John made the bad decision to stay out all night again, I wouldn't accept that. It would be over then. Unfortunately, I found myself half expecting, even waiting for that to happen.

Pastor Gay's counsel would lift my spirits for a few days, but then I'd sink back into the depths of anxiety again. The only way out of this hole I'd dug for myself would be through prayer. I repeated my favorite verses again and again. These verses were my solace, inching out the pain and fear that had previously taken up my thoughts. The Bible taught me to release fear by focusing my mind on my faith. I learned to "set my mind on things above, not on things of this earth" (Colossians 3:2) and that "faith is the substance of things hoped for, the evidence of things not seen" (Hebrews 11:1).

My friends would on occasion invite me out to dinner or an evening prayer service, but even then I was fearful that John might follow me out and find trouble. To avoid opening John up to any kind of temptation, I refused any invitations that came my way. My friends knew that I was just making excuses, but thankfully, they never stopped asking.

I'd fallen back into the role of John's keeper and had forgotten how good it felt to let God help John with his addiction. At least, that was how I saw myself, as the one who had to keep John in line, and when I realized that, I knew I had to let go and let God.

When I stepped back and took a look, I could see all the blessings in my life. Our marriage was growing stronger every day; the boys were thrilled to have their father back in their lives, we belonged to a great church family, we had a lovely home with food on the table every night and more than enough money to live on. Having my family finally give us their support was the icing on the cake.

Trusting God to help us through the dark times allowed me to focus more on the present. When I wasn't looking, a smile snuck onto my face. I was becoming John's wife again in both heart and soul.

I began to make better decisions myself. I knew that God didn't want me to be timid and allow the old fears to control me. Instead, I was making the decision to focus on John's current behavior and his consistent examples of clean living. Saying my newly positive thoughts out loud further strengthened my resolve to embrace this new relationship. "So is my word that goes out from my mouth, it will not return to me empty, but will accomplish what I desire and achieve the purpose for which I sent it" (Isaiah 55:11). I knew that saying Bible verses and my newly forming positive thoughts out loud was giving me power over the negative thoughts that had been monopolizing my thoughts. Once again, God's grace led me to the strength, compassion, and peace that I needed in my life.

# 14
## Chapter

## Still Worried

After John had been home for almost a year, we decided to join my family on the Cape like we had done many times before. I was nervous about being in my parent's company as they were still hesitant about John's ability to toe the line. I carried with me a lot of guilt about what I'd put them through. I know they always had my best interest at heart and they worried a lot about me and the boys. It must have been very hard for them to watch their only daughter and three grandsons go through the ordeals that we did.

My parents and brothers, as well as my extended family, were so gracious and welcoming to us on that vacation. They looked past John's previous struggles and treated us like none of the difficult challenges we faced had ever happened. To this day, my family continues to support me and I am forever grateful.

The vacation proved to be a great time for us to relax and have fun as a family. Over that summer, there were many weekends that we'd drive north to Lake George and spend time fishing and just having fun with the boys. This was the life that we were building together now. Instead of spending his weekends running off with the guys, John was spending time having fun with his family. I was ecstatic, happy for the boys that their father was back in their lives and relieved and excited for myself that my husband was putting our family first.

He found he also wanted to see some changes in his professional life. Working at the autocenter was very different than he'd been used to in his past. The services provided there were limited, as was his role. He longed to open a shop of his own again someday and after many hours discussing it, I was supportive of his dream. John and I began praying about the possibility of opening his own garage in New York and we trusted God would show us the way.

In the meantime, our friends and members of the congregation started asking John to help them with their car troubles. Little by little he began building his reputation as a mechanic. It wasn't obvious to us at first, but God was helping him to build a clientele for the time when he would one day open a garage in the local area.

Around that same time, the lease on our house expired and the landlord wanted to move back home. We loved this house and weren't excited about the additional change this would bring into our lives, but we also trusted that God would again show us the way.

It was difficult to leave Pastor Gay and the house that we'd come to love, but we decided to turn this into another opportunity for us to grow together. We searched the open houses and eventually decided on a lovely home sitting on five acres on Consaul Rd in Colonie, New York. Keeping the boys in the same school district was key for us even if it meant renting a smaller home to live in.

All of our friends came together and helped us move, making it go much smoother than I could have imagined. We settled into our new surroundings and continued to stay in touch with our friends through Sunday service.

The boys were super-excited about our new home and loved playing on all that land. They never doubted for a moment that their dad was home to stay. In the back of my mind I still worried about that.

Even though on the surface it looked like everything was going well, underneath I still worried. I worried a lot. Each time John left the house, I still feared that he would take a drink and slide back down that slippery slope that we all knew led to disaster. I remember him at one point questioning why he couldn't be like the other guys who could stop and have a drink after work and be able to leave after just one. Hearing that, I knew he was still struggling. He was still battling the temptation to drink.

We did find a small garage on Route 7 in Latham, New York to rent. Even though I felt so strongly that he should open up on Central Ave in Colonie, I knew he was getting impatient to be on his own. He kept his job at the autocenter but let them know that he was going to be working at his own place on the weekends. John's Auto Repair took off slowly, but it gave him the confidence to keep following his dream.

Back at the auto center, he was promoted to night supervisor. Working at both garages meant long days for John and he was doing very well for himself. He'd begun to work days and weekends at his own garage and the business was thriving.

# 15
## Chapter

## *A House in Thirty Days*

About that same time, the director from Teen Challenge called to see if the choir could come back to perform at the church. Jimmy V. also mentioned that he'd like to honor John at the service for all that he'd accomplished during the past two years. He wanted to surprise John.

Pastor Gay and I both agreed that this was a great idea. The choir sang beautifully, but the best part was when John was honored in front of his friends and family during service. Everyone was invited to celebrate John's official graduation from Teen Challenge. He received a diploma from Jimmy V. and the congregation acknowledged this victory over addiction with cake after the service.

Life was moving in the right direction and John felt it was time to move to a bigger garage. We'd go for a drive after Church on Sundays, looking for a good location to put an auto repair shop. I was still confident that Central Avenue in Colonie was the best spot to invest in and that is where we focused our attention. On one of those drives, we spotted the ideal location and our path was made clear to the owner of the building. Again God showed us favor and with very little effort we had a signed lease in our hands.

I knew that the Bible is the anointed word of God. One of my favorite verses, Proverbs 3:5 reminds us to trust the Lord with all our heart and in all our ways. To acknowledge Him and He will direct our path. John and I prayed that scripture multiple times and once again our prayers were answered. We felt strongly that with God's guidance, we were moving in the right direction. We were grateful when the clientele he'd built up followed him to this new location.

Three years after graduation from the Teen Challenge program, John decided to give his notice at the auto center. He wanted to devote his time to building up his own garage. His business continued to grow with a great location and he decided to apply for a dealer license to also sell cars.

Our relationship was also growing stronger. We had a lot more in common, primarily our involvement with the Church. John had become the vice president and eventually president of the men's ministry and I was president of the women's ministry. We spent our time assisting others on their spiritual journeys and became closer ourselves through that process. There is something very appealing about a man who loves God.

My guard was no longer up. My trust had been slowly restored and my fears that he would relapse had lessened. I had grown to respect the man I married once again. The kids were involved in youth group and were growing in leaps and bounds. We were all learning to put the past behind us.

As the date approached for the second renewal of our lease, the landlord notified us that he was moving back home. After just a few years, we were going to have to find another place to live again. We asked God to guide us to a home in the same district again.

Much to our surprise, we had thirty days to vacate our home. At the same time, I was told that I needed surgery on my throat. My doctor was in Boston and that's where we planned the surgery. While I was in Boston for two weeks, John was busy with our sons and looking for our next home.

It was my hope that we could avoid the boys changing schools again and John was trying desperately to locate a house nearby. He spotted an ad in the paper for a house that was for sale just a few blocks away and he called the builder to inquire about renting it. After listening to more of John's story, the builder suggested that John take a walk through the house and call him afterward.

John went over to the house and was amazed by what he saw. It was a beautiful, brand new house that was just getting the finishing touches. He called the builder back right away and let him know he was interested in renting. And just like that we had a house and were moved in within thirty days.

After moving into the new house and with the boys getting older, I was ready to work outside of the home again. I continued the daycare center, but also accepted a part-time job working nights at the makeup counter at a nearby department store.

# 16
## Chapter

## *The Accident*

O ne night that muggy August, we were planning to attend evening service as a family, but John let me know he was running late from work. He still planned to join us, but I started feeling uneasy. I didn't hear any more from him and remembered from past experience that no news was *never* good news.

Dinner came and went without John making it home. I explained to the boys that their dad had to work late and we were skipping evening service that week. The boys didn't seem to mind and went outside to play with their neighborhood friends. I stayed inside with my stomach doing summersaults. My calls to the garage went unanswered.

When bedtime came, I tucked the boys in and tried to think positive thoughts. I went out to the living room and began praying in earnest. I prayed that the Holy Spirit watch over John and bring him home safely to me. As much as I prayed, I was still haunted with memories of our past when John made poor decisions. Oh, how I hoped that wasn't the case this time.

Just the night before, I suspected that John had a drink after work. When I asked him about it, he denied it. For the first time in a long time, I didn't believe his words and told him that he was playing with fire and he was going to get burned. We could all get burned. We ended up having a heated argument over it and we really didn't resolve anything by the time we went to bed. I let him know that I believed he was making bad choices and that he wasn't the only one being impacted by those choices. We argued about it, but I continued to trust God to watch over him, knowing it wasn't my job to do so. Just the same, I was in a lot of turmoil over it and afraid of history repeating itself.

I found out later that John would occasionally stop at a bar after work and have a beer to wind down with some of his friends from the auto center. It seemed like he didn't understand why I had an issue with his grabbing a beer on the way home from work. He thought that as long as he came home, he was doing everything he needed to. He expected me to believe he only had one drink and that there was no problem. He was back in denial. I didn't see it that way and made sure he knew how I felt.

I wasn't going to go down that path again. I wasn't getting back on that merry-go-round of pain and anxiety. We had built a good life here in Albany. I didn't want John to throw it all away on a couple of drinks. I was afraid he was losing control.

I prayed even more, this time for the children. Aged 14, 12, and 10, they needed their father sober and in their lives. I went to bed after that, the Bible at my side. In the past, I'd been able to fall asleep, but I couldn't find solace in sleep that night. Alone in bed, all I could think about was that something had happened to John. I was trying to give him the benefit of the doubt and think that it wasn't related to drinking. It had been so many years since he'd fallen prey to his addiction. I really hoped that wasn't happening now.

After a period of time, I gave up on sleep and headed out to the kitchen where I prayed more. The phone rang around midnight. Straight out of a nightmare, I heard John's voice at the other end screaming at me. He yelled that he was afraid he'd killed someone.

My mind couldn't process the words I was hearing from him and I tried to focus on the facts. He told me he was in a phone booth somewhere on Central Avenue and he had just walked away from a head-on collision.

He assured me that he wasn't seriously injured, but he was afraid that three young girls in the other car might have been. He wanted me to come there as quickly as possible to help him. I wasn't able to respond. My legs got weak and my stomach turned. I couldn't wrap my head around it. Could this be real? Could John, the man I had worked so hard to trust again, be responsible for the deaths of three innocent girls?

I pulled myself together with all the inner strength I could muster and threw on a pair of jeans. I wrote a quick note to the boys telling them their dad's car had broken down and I was going to get him. Then, I called one of John's friends, Will, that knew about his history. I wasn't sure what I was going to find at the accident scene and I needed support. Our friend agreed to go with me and I picked him up on the way.

The mugginess hadn't lifted, even that late at night, making it difficult to breathe. As we drove up on the accident scene, I was reminded of that horrific night four winters before. There were flashing blue and red lights surrounding the mangled vehicles in the road and I was certain that I'd find John restrained in cuffs.

Emergency vehicles blocked my access to the scene and police told me that I had to stay back. I was determined to find out what was going on, navigated through the mess to get a closer look, and then I saw his car. In the back of my mind, I was hoping against hope that this nightmare wasn't the accident John had been involved in.

It didn't become real until I saw John's sedan, smashed where he had crossed the double yellow lines. The other car looked to have taken the bulk of the impact. A Volkswagon Jetta, driven by a young woman, was just a small car and not enough to sustain the force behind John's Lincoln Towncar. Jaws of life were in use as they tried to free a trapped passenger in that little car. People were beginning to gather, watching the accident scene like it was some kind of cheap entertainment.

I found my way to the officer standing near the other car and asked if the passengers in the second car were alright. Again, the officer tried to force me back, but I explained my husband had been the driver of the sedan. His tone went from bad to worse as the officer told me that John had been arrested and I'd have to listen to the news to see if everyone in the second car survived.

His anger toward me, seeing me as guilty by association, was enough to turn me away. Without actually seeing John, I climbed back into my car with the intention of heading to Ben's house, one of John's business associates. Will stayed with me and when I stopped the car and began banging on the steering wheel because I couldn't take it any more, he pushed me out of the driver's seat and drove us to John's business associate's house.

We called Pastor Gay at 1:00am from Ben's house and I tried to explain what happened. I was hysterical and Pastor Gay did his best to calm me and said quietly to me, "Michelle, listen to me, I'm not surprised to receive your call." He went on to recite Romans 8:28 to me, "And we know that in all things, God works for the good of those who love him, who have been called according to his purpose." What Pastor Gay didn't know was that very verse had crossed through my mind several times that day and night. It even came to mind in the car on the way to the scene of the accident. When I heard those words from Pastor Gay, I began to calm down.

Pastor Gay shared with me that he'd been prompted by the Holy Spirit to pray for John around 11:00 that night with such an urgency that he hadn't been able to shake the uneasy feeling himself. We prayed together for John and Pastor Gay promised to pick me up in the morning so that we could attend John's arraignment together. I was incredibly grateful for Pastor Gay's support and for the peace and calm that the Holy Spirit bestowed upon me, even during this time of extreme chaos.

Will came back to the house with me. Thankfully, the boys were still asleep. Unfortunately, I left in such a panic that I didn't grab my house keys and now had no way to get back in. My nerves were shot. One part of me wanted to hit John with all my might, hurting him like he was hurting me. I walked around my house looking for an open window that I could use to crawl inside but to no avail.

Eventually, I rang the doorbell and braced myself to see my sleepy-eyed sons, having to explain why I was outside in the middle of the night with no key. Fortunately, Ryan, our middle son, wasn't quite awake when he opened the door and, after seeing me, turned and headed back to his room.

I asked Will to stay at the house that night for support. He agreed to watch the early morning news for an update on everyone's condition.

I wasn't up to hearing John's name on the news again. I thought that was all behind us, but instead, our world was crashing down around us. The boys and I were going to have to deal with the aftermath of John's actions again.

Exhausted and numb, I crawled into bed and tried to sleep. There was no rest for me, however, and I watched time on the clock creep slowly ahead. Worry for those young girls plagued my mind. I trusted Will to give me the update as soon as he heard. We had to make sure the television was turned off before the boys awoke. I didn't want them finding out that way.

Later that morning, I found out that there was no report of the accident on the early morning news. There was no real relief gained by that, but I was glad I didn't have to tell the boys yet. There was a strong chance that news of John's involvement wouldn't have made it to the boys' schools yet. I thought we'd be safe waiting to tell them until we knew more about the situation.

Pastor Gay came by at 8am. The boys had already gone off to school. We headed to the courthouse in Schenectady, New York and both of my brothers agreed to meet us there. We found out that John was charged with a DWI, leaving the scene of an accident and vehicular assault. My brothers helped John make bail and he was released on his own recognizance. Pastor Gay and I brought him home.

Despite my anger broiling on the inside, I remained loving and caring on the outside. I tried to keep in mind that John never intended for this chaos and destruction to enter our lives. At home, he filled me in on the details. He explained that he'd gone to the bar in order to meet a man about possibly purchasing a car lot that was available. He'd remembered his commitment to attend church that night and planned to only be there for a few minutes.

He agreed to have a drink with the man and that cold beer went down smoothly. From there, he didn't stop. He had another and, before he knew it, four hours had passed. By the time he left, he was inebriated and hungry. He didn't actually remember leaving the bar, but he did go in search of food. The next thing he remembered was colliding head-on with those three young girls. He did leave the scene, but only to call me.

The police report stated that John was traveling between 45 and 50 miles per hour while going west from Central Ave onto State Street where he fell asleep for about 20 seconds. Those 20 seconds were all it took to cross those yellow lines. When he woke up, he tugged on the steering wheel, trying to correct his mistake and get back to his side of the road, but wasn't able to avoid the impact. The woman driving in the oncoming lane had also tried to turn away, heading in the same direction as John had.

The right front engines of both cars collided. Airbags deployed and John was dazed by the impact. He jumped out of the car and could hear the girls' screams. The police and ambulance arrived at the scene. In a panic, he ran to the pay phone a block down the street and called me. He wanted to make sure I heard it from him and not from some strange policeman knocking at my door. After that, John sat down on the sidewalk where the police found him all banged up and asked if he'd been involved in the accident. They threw handcuffs on him and took him to the station to book him.

I was confused and angry. In all honesty, I was even angry at God. I'd been sure that our lives had moved past this kind of nightmarish hell. I was filled with disappointment. I felt like I'd been betrayed yet again. How could John have made a decision to put himself in the position to be tempted? All I could think of was our kids.

I never really committed to helping John through this ordeal. It was more like I was numb and just went through the motions. One foot in front of the other, but at each step I questioned whether I was doing the right thing by staying with him.

We still hadn't told the boys what had happened and somehow managed to make it to their football game that evening. We tried to go about our daily routines while we waited for an update on the condition of the girls in the other car. It seemed that they were all alive and we were grateful for that. I believed that the all-night prayers of our friends had something to do with that.

John and I weren't sure how things were going to end up. We were walking on eggshells. We knew it wasn't going to be good, but we kept praying for the best it could be. The most important thing was that those girls be alright. We'd handle whatever the law threw at us.

I surprised myself by sticking with John. For so long, I'd thought that I wouldn't put up with anything that remotely resembled our past life. As bad as it was, this seemed different. John wasn't running away from his life by using drugs and alcohol this time. I truly believed that he just didn't understand the control that they had over him. He mistakenly thought he could control his urge to have a beer, stopping whenever he wanted. He thought he could be just like one of the guys, stopping for a quick beer and a word with a potential business partner. He learned the hard way that wasn't the case.

# 17
## Chapter

## Something Inside of Me Changed

The church was very supportive of us, but we felt it best to resign from our leadership duties for the men and women's ministries. We needed to focus our attention closer to home. Our knowledge of the girls' condition was limited, but we continued to pray for their recovery. We did learn that two of the three were treated and released from the hospital shortly after the accident, but one remained hospitalized. The last we knew, she was in critical condition.

My brother recommended an attorney that specialized in representing those who were charged with DWIs. The attorney was very expensive and John had set his mind to pleading guilty to all charges, regardless of the attorney's advice. John was willing to face the consequences of his actions.

While I didn't want to see John convicted and sent to jail for his actions, I understood his need to be accountable and that was something I could stand behind. That was the John who I loved. Life wouldn't be easy with him in prison, but we both expected that would be the outcome.

Over the next few weeks, John met with his attorney but still refused to agree to anything less than a guilty plea. His attorney was confident that he could get a reduced charge, but John stood strong in his need for accountability. How well the third girl recovered from her injuries would also play a role in the sentence that John would receive, but her progress was still unknown to us.

I continued to put one foot in front of the other and tried to carry on as if life weren't spiraling out of control. I was reminded of 1 Chronicles 16:11, "Look to the Lord and His strength; seek his face always." My faith kept me strong. We carried on our daily routines as usual and kept the worry of tomorrow tucked away, out of reach of our boys, as best we could.

There were months of waiting for the legal process to play out. We spent countless nights discussing possible outcomes and we leaned on one another in ways that we never had before. There was something inside of me that changed during that period of time. I found that life wasn't all hugs and smiles. No, real life had its ups and downs. The difference was that with faith, those downs didn't mean hitting rock bottom. God's love was the cushion that softened our fall and the light that lit our way to rise once again.

The anger that continued to broil internally spilled over from time to time. There was no denying that John's actions had a huge negative impact on not only his life but on the lives of the boys and me. It was difficult to get by that without my anger surfacing. John understood and took the brunt of my anger without striking back in kind. He listened to my sharp words and kept apologizing for causing my pain. Not once did he shirk his responsibility for drinking that evening. Even when I had moments of despising him, I couldn't help but respect that.

We still hadn't told my parents what had happened. I was glad that they were living in Boston and hadn't heard it on the news. Eventually, we'd have to tell them, but we delayed as long as possible. We wanted to have a better idea of what John might be facing before we shared the unpleasant news with them.

After three months passed, there was a report released telling us that the third girl had awakened from her coma and was being transferred to a rehabilitation center for further healing. The best news was that she was expected to make a full recovery. John and I rejoiced when we heard that.

Christmas that year had an undercurrent of tension. My parents still didn't know what had happened and we tried to keep things as normal as possible for the boys. Winter in New York was bad enough, but dark thoughts of John heading off to prison in handcuffs brought me down even further. I couldn't imagine how John was feeling but was pleased that he hadn't turned to chemical substances to get him through it. We both leaned on our faith to help us survive it.

We headed to court in early January 1997. John would finally have a chance to enter his guilty plea. It was then that the sentencing court date was set for March 31$^{st}$ and we had to prepare for what that might bring.

After court, we headed to the Parole department so John could be deposed. Pastor Gay stayed with us through it all. The deposition took about three hours and we were all exhausted at the conclusion. While we were there, we found out that the three girls had lawyers and we wondered if they would be in court on the 31$^{st}$ of March. John hoped so because he wanted to apologize to them in person.

I couldn't imagine what they might say to John. I wondered if they would forgive him or if they'd be angry with him. Who could blame them if they were angry with John? Anger still creeped into my life now and again. I worried, however, that if they spoke angrily at John, it could hurt his case and cause an even harsher sentence.

John's attorney encouraged us to get as many letters of reference that we could. We needed to highlight his good character that was being overshadowed by this ugly event. We reached out to church members, family members, business associates, and close friends who were all more than happy to speak well of John.

Now that the time was upon us, John insisted that we sit down as a family and discuss life after sentencing. There was no doubt that John would be heading to prison for an indeterminate amount of time. Where I would just blindly lean on God for help, John felt it was important to have a plan in place. He wanted to make sure that we had support lined up to help us through the tough days ahead.

That Easter, we traveled to Boston to celebrate with my parents. It was March 30th and we still hadn't told my parents. I felt bad about that but didn't want to spoil our last weekend together as a family.

Monday morning, March 31st, John's court date arrived. I watched him in the bathroom straightening his tie. I felt a tug at my heartstrings. He was so handsome, but I could see a mask of shame across his face. He knew he had to pay his dues for the poor decisions he made. I could see a real change in his personality from years past. He'd gone from somewhat arrogant and selfish to what I saw as a humbled man. This older, more mature version of my husband was much more attractive to me than the more cocky man that he was in his youth.

Once we were both ready to go, as ready as we could be, we headed to court in the midst of a snow storm. There, I glanced around; I saw three women together on the other side of the room and surmised they were those involved in the accident. As I stared at the backs of their heads, I remembered all the prayers that we said for them. We prayed time and again that their lives would resume normalcy and not be changed because of the accident. I was certain these women and their families felt the same kind of agony these past few months that my family did. I prayed to myself, "let there be peace among us." The judge entered the courtroom and everyone stood. The proceedings began.

My thoughts turned to the letters written by our friends and those John had professional relationships with. These folks wrote about how John had been a positive role model in his church, business, and community. Even more people wrote about our sons' and John's relationship with them and love for them. They went on to also talk about the strength of our marriage and our having remained together during sometimes troubled times in our past. A letter from Pastor Gay spoke of John's faithful membership at his church and service on several committees. He referenced John's opening our home to those needing mentorship, especially to those recovering from addiction. Some talked about the role he played for others who needed love and attention and an understanding of how to believe in oneself. There were several letters from recovered addicts that attested to John's contribution in helping them along their own paths to recovery. I wondered if the judge would be influenced at all by these letters of reference. Would the judge be able to visualize all the good John had brought to the community or would he only see the damage that had been brought that awful night where those three young women were sent to the hospital?

With the proceedings underway, I tried to concentrate on what was happening in the courtroom, but my mind kept traveling to the potential outcome. I was so frightened by what I imagined I might face in my future. I heard the judge speak to the three women and request that they provide their comments on what happened and their feelings about John's sentencing. My brother Joe and his wife Martha were in the courtroom, along with my brother Stephen, neighbors, and Pastor Gay.

My mind shutdown. My hands got clammy and I felt like I was having a hot flash. I didn't know if I could sit through their testimonies. I just wanted to block it all out. I wanted to wake up from this nightmare. I couldn't imagine that anything they said would help John. I knew they had every right to tell their stories, but I just didn't know if I could listen. My whole life flashed in front of me and I wanted to run far away from that courtroom.

I was stunned when I heard the women's attorney speak up and ask for leniency in this case. I almost fell over. The attorney went on to explain that they were aware of John's contributions to the community and his strong family relationships. They knew John had a family to care for and wanted the judge to be lenient when sentencing.

From there, the judge spoke to John, asking if he had any remarks to share. I held my breath and listened for John. "Yes, your honor," John said. "I want to sincerely apologize to each victim here today." Then, he turned to look at the three women, "I am truly sorry for my actions. I am sorry you were hurt so terribly." Next, he looked at me, "Michelle, I apologize to you and our boys and our whole extended family, to our church family, my customers, and anyone else I let down or hurt by my actions. I take full responsibility for my actions."

There was silence in the courtroom. After John was sent back to take his seat at the defendant's table, the judge gave his closing words. "I have before me a stack of letters from people of this community testifying to Mr. Mulledy's character and asking me for leniency. It is clear to me that he is an outstanding individual. He has touched the lives of many people for the better and is a productive citizen, husband, and father. It is days like this that I really don't enjoy my job. This situation could happen to any one of us that are gathered here today. We could go out, have a few drinks, get into our car and drive home, not realizing we had too much to drink. We mean no harm to anyone, but, unfortunately, our senses are dulled and we cause an accident. Mr. Mulledy has pled guilty and has taken full responsibility; however, I must uphold the law because this is a very serious offense. I sentence John Mulledy for a sentence of 1 to 3 years in a state correctional facility. He is to be turned over immediately to the department of correctional services within the state of New York." The judge sealed John's fate with a strike of his gavel and stood to leave the courtroom.

I exhaled a long breath. I felt my legs go weak and I was glad to have Pastor Gay, my family and close friends around me. John turned to look at me and I saw the smile on his face. Even with his hands bound and being escorted out of the courtroom, I could see that he was still the love my life.

With John gone, I felt compelled to talk to the three women. I made my way to the other side of the courtroom. "Excuse me," I said, struggling to find my voice through all of the emotions. "I am so sorry this happened to you." I couldn't say any more as those emotions completely took me over. The women were very kind to me and assured me that they were all fine.

I tried to hold it together as the court officers found me and handed over John's clothing and other belongings in a large plastic bag. That's when I saw him. John was dressed in an orange prison jumpsuit with his ankles shackled and hands cuffed. He was being led out of the building and I guessed he was headed to a penitentiary somewhere in New York.

I can't even begin to express what that felt like. Somehow this was even worse than when John was arrested in Boston. I knew we'd get through this, but it was difficult to see him that way. I looked over at Pastor Gay and knew my faith and faith community would be there for me and my family.

Seven months of worry were now behind us. John was ready to pay his debt to society, and as bad as it was, we could now begin to see a light at the end of the tunnel. No longer was a dark cloud hanging over us, waiting to hear what the sentence would be. Now, we could start crossing the days until John would come back home and be with his family again. As empty as I felt inside right then, I also felt a strong sense of relief.

That part of the tragedy of that night was now behind us and we could start looking to the future again.

Like I'd been planning to, I called my parents when I got home from the sentencing. Of course, it was a shock to them. They wanted to come to Albany to help comfort the boys and me, but I assured them they didn't need to. With my brother Joe and Martha spending the night, I thought we'd be fine. My 8 month old niece, Lauren stayed over as well, bringing with her the laughter and joy that only a baby can bring. Having that distraction was a blessing. I thought the first night would be the roughest, but really, I was still pretty numb then. My sister-in-law Martha was a source of encouragement to me and both of my brothers were there whenever I needed to lean on them.

In the next couple of days, after my brother and his family left, I fell into depression. Even though I knew John never intended for this to happen, I couldn't help but feel let down by him. There had been a part of me that feared he would slip back into his old ways and I had tried so hard to let that go. I knew he didn't fall solidly back into the old John's habits, but he had started on a slippery slope that was disastrous. There were some days where I even thought it was probably a good thing this happened. If he hadn't hit a wall, I fear where he might have ended up.

Some days, I even questioned God. I couldn't understand, after all that we had gone through and all that John had gone through as a child, how we could keep ending up in the same spot. At times, I wondered if my decision to stay with John was the right one. Other times, I knew it was John's introducing me to Jesus and my new faith that made the difference in my life. It was my Christian faith that kept leading me back to a place of calm, a place of peace.

I knew that the decisions we made were our own. We are blessed with freedom of choice. As such, I knew it was John's decision, not God's that placed him in prison. I also knew that God would be there for us no matter what. No matter how many poor decisions any of us might make, God would be there holding out His arms to support us through the consequences of our choices.

I recognized that it would be another challenge for me as well as our boys. The boys no longer could ignore what occurred around them. They'd have to deal with people knowing that their father was incarcerated. Sometimes I thought about how differently they were growing up than I did. My father was always there for me. I never had to worry whether he was coming home at night or whether he was going off to prison. I had no way of knowing what kind of impact John's situation would have on our sons, but again, I had to turn this fear over to the Lord. I prayed that God would protect our sons from any chance of substance that might draw them and from any negative impact that the instability we've faced might have on their psyches.

I had known since the night of the accident that my faith was shaken. It felt like benign tumors that never kill me but place more and more fear in my heart with every new growth. It was a roller coaster of emotions. When it came right down to it, even on my worst days, I still trusted God to see me through.

Day to day, I tried to hang on but felt myself getting psychically weaker. Was I heading toward a mental breakdown? Sometimes I wondered. I knew I had to be strong for the boys, but the pain and emptiness I felt from the weight of depression was becoming too much for me. I sought medical attention and had a plethora of tests run. No physical ailment was found, which confirmed my doctor's suspicion that I was battling the symptoms of full on depression.

For me, depression meant everything was ten times harder than before. I felt like there were weights on my limbs and I could barely lift them to do anything. It was difficult to get out of bed in the morning. I was exhausted no matter how long I might have slept.

There were days that I was overcome with loneliness which turned into a cycle of anger and back to depression. My life had become almost unbearable for me. Thank God for the boys. I kept moving because of them. I also kept going to church. God's word also kept me going. It was hard to hear the encouraging words from well-meaning friends and church members. The words just echoed in the hollowness inside me. After service, I'd run from church seeking the safety of my home.

When the landlord came in April to collect his rent, he could tell something was wrong. I explained what had happened with John and that he'd be away in prison for a while. After listening to my story, the man who built and owned our lovely home, Jack, handed me back the check I'd given him. He declared that I would not pay him rent for the duration of John's sentence. In disbelief, I made him repeat what he said. I explained that my husband likely wouldn't be back for at least two years.

He did not want me to worry about having to provide a home for our boys while John did his time. Before he left, he turned to me and said, "Thank God, not me." I was stunned. I kept saying, "thank you," over and over again.

God just performed another miracle in my life. I wasn't going to have to worry about paying the rent while John was away. My boys could stay in their beautiful home and wouldn't be uprooted because I didn't have enough money to pay our rent. God was providing for us just like Psalms 132:15a reads, "I will bless her with abundant provisions."

While the rent was being provided for, John's business was another story all together. John had hired someone to manage the business while he was incarcerated, but unfortunately, the business didn't seem to be withstanding the change. Just like before, John and his personality was the reason for success. Without him, the business was flailing. We ended up closing the shop before the end of the year was out. We didn't want to close it but couldn't see any other way around it. John was going to have to start all over again when he was released.

John was placed in a minimum security facility three hours away. When I first visited him, I barely recognized him. His head had been shaved and in a few days he looked like he'd aged a few years. He told me that the admittance procedures were awful. Even though I was already exhausted, I normally drove three hours to see him on the weekends when I could. I would often contemplate my life circumstances on those long drives. I gave the boys the option to join me if they wanted. They were mature enough to make that decision on their own and I didn't want to make them feel they were being punished or forced to go. I told John that he made the decision that put him in the situation that he was in and the boys were not going to miss out on spending birthdays and holidays with their family. I told him that they were not going to suffer for the mistakes that he made and the situation he found himself in. We were allowed to bring John food, books, letters and other incidentals that brought him some pleasure during his isolation.

The visits themselves weren't pleasant. Our conversations tended to be heavy and tense. They were filled with me giving him ultimatums about what would happen when he came home. I told him often that the girl he'd married more than thirty years ago was long gone. In her place was a very disheartened, disappointed, and disillusioned woman. Even with Jesus in my heart the days were difficult.

It was a very different feeling than when he was in the Teen Challenge program. Back then, I'd been very excited and welcomed the positive changes that were happening in my life. I was older now, my life was established, and I resented John for putting our family and the life we'd built together in this awful position of dealing with his poor choices.

There was rarely a day that went by that I didn't feel embarrassed or different because of John being incarcerated. Being a single mom wasn't so bad. Society accepted that without a blink of an eye, but having a husband in prison left one with a stigma. I felt like people considered John's actions to be dishonorable actions and that rubbed off on me. Somehow, by the grace of God, I'm sure, I started to get stronger. The weight of depression began to lift a little. My days were still split between the daycare and my part-time job at the local department store where I sold cosmetics. Those children I watched in the daycare cheered me up when I most needed it. Even though I didn't have a large group anymore, I still needed assistance and my friend Jackie lent a hand. Most days were filled to the brim with my jobs and caring for the boys, and with whatever time was left spent staying on top of the housework. It was important to me that I keep things unchanged for the boys wherever I could, even if it was just small things like keeping the house clean.

In prison, John attended Alcoholics Anonymous. He spent his time being a witness for Christ and helping the other inmates find their way. He was dubbed the nickname 'Rev.' The feeling of peace and contentment came upon him once again. He spent his days working within the prison and his nights in Bible study with other like minded inmates in his dorm. He shared the food I brought with these men, feeling sorry for those who didn't have regular visitors like he did. He told me that whenever he made coffee in the small pot they let him keep in his room, fellow inmates would come running. Focusing on the positive, he offered anyone who came for Bible study in his room a cup of hot coffee. It was a win-win. The inmates got fresh coffee and John got to spread the word of God.

Yet again, God was working through John. Yes, even in prison, John was doing God's work. I could see the positive actions John was taking, but I still harbored resentment for his being imprisoned. I wanted him home sharing the word of God with the boys and me. Was I being selfish? I didn't care.

Many times I sat in that visiting room, shocked that I was living that reality. Anger and resentment welled up inside of me. I was angry at John for putting us in this situation. Still, I kept that resentment and anger hidden. I didn't want to make a bad situation worse. I could see John taking responsibility for what he'd done and trying to make something good come of it. I kept my feelings to myself, myself and God.

By Christmastime John was incarcerated for nine months. I loved Christmas in my youth, but now I dreaded the holiday. The boys and I would be spending another Christmas without John. I could bring myself to visit John on the holiday, but John and I agreed that it was better to keep the holiday positive for the boys and not have them spend the day in a prison visitation room. Instead, we spent Christmas with my family and, by myself I visited John the day after.

There was excitement in John's voice when I got there. He was closing in on twelve months in prison and would soon be eligible for parole. We were both surprised to learn that the same judge who sentenced him also sent a letter to the parole board on John's behalf.

With fervor, John read to me from the judge's letter, "In my fifteen years in the criminal justice system, I know of only one other case which generated for a defendant the quantity and quality of sincere support from individuals in the community as this one. The letters that were submitted to me on Mr. Mulledy's behalf demonstrated the positive effect of his life on those around him. I ask that the Board of Parole take a good look, hard look at the pre-sentencing memorandum that incorporates a selection of those letters and which I directed be made part of the correctional file." The judge continued, "It was my responsibility in March to administer a sentence for what I believe was a low point in Mr. Mulledy's life. He appears to have the type of family and community support that are essential to success in life after a period of incarceration, and I expect that the high point of his life is in his future. I wouldn't oppose a decision by the Board granting his release."

If John was paroled he would likely be a candidate for a local work-release program. Just the thought of leaving prison and living with his family again lit up John's face, but it was hard for me to get my hopes up about a potentially imminent release. It did give John something to look forward to, but I wasn't sure what his odds of release really were and I didn't want to be let down again. In my heart of hearts, I didn't think he'd be coming home that soon.

When the time came, the parole board reviewed the letters originally provided in reference to John's character at the trial as well as the letter written by the judge. They also considered John's good behavior while serving his time, but as I feared, their decision weighed against releasing John. It wasn't all bad news, however, since they decided to move John to a prison that was only thirty minutes from home.

His second year in prison was much the same, just a little bit closer. My daily routines weren't really impacted. Whenever I visited John, it seemed like we'd get into really intense conversations and they weren't all good. There was a lot of rehashing the past and equal time spent talking about the future. The closer it got to the time for the second parole review board, the greater the intensity in our conversations. We talked a lot about what was right and wrong. There was a part of me that still feared John could make a wrong decision like the one that landed him there in prison. I encouraged him to stay close to God and be the man that our boys expect him to be.

After the second year in prison was completed, I suspected that John would be paroled. I wondered how we would adjust to living together again. For two years, we'd lived without one another in our daily lives. There was no doubt in my mind that we'd have some ups and downs before we found a comfortable routine again.

I hoped that the boys wouldn't face negative feedback from their peers when John came back on the scene. It was a lot for my young men to handle. I did speak to the principals of their schools when the accident happened. They assured me that they would keep an eye out for the boys. I needed to be sure that other students wouldn't harass them because of their father's actions. Thankfully, my fears were unfounded and none of their schoolmates or friends gave them a hard time about what happened.

I wasn't sure how I would react myself to John's coming back home. I'm a strong woman who grew even stronger during John's two years of incarceration and I didn't know what it would be like to share my life with him again. I was used to calling the shots and having control. Introducing John back into the daily mix of things would feel like losing some of that control. I wasn't sure I really wanted that. There was a part of me that was afraid of what could happen if I wasn't in control. In my heart I knew that God is in control, but my humanness caused me to worry about the reunion with John. A part of me knew that our faith in God would help us conquer anything we might encounter during the transition. Like always, however, it was hard not knowing the answers up front and having to rely on the unknown to get us through.

Sure enough, after serving two-thirds of his sentence, John was granted a release. His first concern was finding a job now that he was a convicted felon. He didn't think his chances were good at landing something that was comparable to what he had before he lost it all. He wouldn't even be able to drive when he got out. His discouragement was palpable. I tried the best I could to be supportive of him and encouraging, but I honestly thought that was going to be a difficult task too.

During one of our intense conversations, going around in circles about the same old things, John looked away and smiled. We were both surprised to see his old boss, Paul from the autocenter walking into the room. It was the first time he'd been to visit John during his incarceration. When he sat down next to me, he seemed genuinely happy to see John. He inquired about John's plans when he was released. He'd heard that John was being released soon and wanted to let him know that there was a spot for John at the autocenter if he was interested. We were both in shock. John had a job waiting for him if he wanted it.

Hallelujah! It was difficult to believe what I was hearing, but God was coming through for us again. His former boss hoped he'd consider coming back to work for him. We didn't know how Paul had heard he was being released, but we were grateful that he'd found out. Another of our prayers had been answered.

Thankfully, John's transition home wasn't as intense as his Teen Challenge homecoming. This time, we were older and with age came grace. I was determined to dismiss any unwanted stares by others and ignore any gossip that might be spread about us. I embraced the opportunity to fall in love with my husband again and learned not to preach to him but instead fully believe in the word of God.

John took full responsibility for his addiction to alcohol and drugs. I'd made it very clear during our prison visits that he needed to steer clear of any temptation he might face, or we were finished. I was not going to allow myself to ever again be dragged into the type of situation we'd just lived though. I had my own mental health and our sons' health to consider. That was my responsibility to care for myself instead of putting John first. I wouldn't choose to be a part of his poor choices in the future. I'd already given him a second chance and he understood there wouldn't be a third.

# 18
## Chapter

# Ever After

The first year of our reunion I found myself emotionally in a place similar to when John came home from Teen Challenge. I was very anxious regarding our ability to reconnect and maintain a stable home for our children. On the outside I looked cool as a cucumber, but on the inside, I was nervous and afraid to trust my husband to become the head of the household again. I had fallen into that role during John's absence and was afraid to hand over the reins again.

It was important for me to press into God more than ever during this time. I'd heard promises from John before and was afraid to believe them another time. Instead, I leaned on my faith and a new trust I'd found for my own self and my ability to discern the truth.

I spent a lot of time on my knees praying and looking for answers in the Bible. I frequently recited Romans 8:28, "For we know that all things work together for the good of those who love God and who are called according to His purpose." When I considered the word "all" in this verse, it reminded me that more than just the good things work toward the purpose of God. It helped me to see that difficult times could also be part of God's purpose!

I was determined to find peace within the household, my relationship with John, and with our children. Most importantly, I had to find peace within myself as I often found myself questioning my decision to reunite with John when he was released from prison. It was so easy to second-guess myself. I was also constantly on guard against falling into past behaviors that I'd since learned were unhealthy. Like I had in the past, I stepped into the role of guardian for the family. I would do everything I could to keep the kids and myself from being hurt again.

I prayed non-stop that God would watch over my children and see that my kids were happy and continue to have their father in their lives. At times when the internal battle sapped my strength and I didn't want to get out of bed, I'd often turned back to Proverbs 3:5-6, "Trust in the Lord with all your heart and do not rely on your own understanding. In all your ways acknowledge Him and He will make your path straight."

When I considered Jesus instructing Peter to leave the boat in Matthew 14:27-32, I applied that instruction to my own life. I needed to step out of the comfort zone of my boat into the unknown. I understood that if I turned away from Jesus, fear would overtake me. With the strength of this knowledge, I was able to, over time, share family and household responsibilities again and allow John to more fully be my partner.

My church was a great help to me and another great source of strength before and after John returned home. Pastor Gay and his wife Joyce were truly a spiritual covering for me. Like a warm blanket, their care brought me a sense of security during very challenging times. I knew I wasn't alone. Their relationship was an example of the harmony Jesus could create in a marriage. John did accept the position at the autocenter when he was released. Shortly after that, he was offered and accepted the position of District Manager, a position that he'd coveted in the past. The position held oversight responsibilities of 11 different autocenters in the northeast and required frequent travel. The travel made me nervous, but I knew I had to turn it over to God. From there, he was offered an even higher position as District Manager for Sears Logistics. It was this position that led him to the job he is in now as a manager for a national logistics company.

As the path of our life together changed, we transitioned to Victory Christian Church where Pastor Charlie Muller presided. It was through Pastor Charlie that we also met Pastor Marty Stanton and we became part of the ministry team the two oversaw. Together, we served the population at Albany County Jail on Sunday nights. John and I both spoke individually to the inmates, speaking to female and male inmates separately. This ministry is just one of the ways that John's and my worlds began to reconnect.

Over the years, John and I have both met with individuals and couples having faced similar challenges with drugs and alcohol. It is important to us that we share God's word with others and help them with our testimonies. Rather than try to forget or hide the issues we've dealt with through the years, we have found that through this sharing of our own story, we have greatly improved our marriage. We knew that God didn't cause our issues, but we also knew that we could use these troubling times to glorify His kingdom. We give others hope and act as living proof of God's restorative power.

It is our wish that others seek God for understanding of how His word can best be applied in their own lives. There is no magic formula as we are all individual reflections of God and each unique in our own ways. This is my story and how I found my path to peace. I would never encourage someone in an abusive relationship to remain in a dangerous situation. I pray that others who read this story lean on their faith and ask for the wisdom of the Holy Spirit to guide them on their path forward.

John and I will celebrate our 42$^{nd}$ wedding anniversary in September of this year. Our three sons are living healthy productive lives and we have 4 beautiful grandsons.

We continue to attend Victory Christian Church in Colonie, New York and our relationship continues to be enriched by our shared faith in God, the Holy Spirit, and Christ.

It is only through God's grace that we have navigated the treacherous waters that came our way. Faith carried me when I didn't have the strength to go on; the Holy Spirit guided me when I was lost.

I'm grateful for the lessons that I learned through the years and I'm happy to now know myself in a way that I'd not known in my younger days. Feeling blessed, spending my days with the man who captured my heart so long ago, I look forward to the next chapter of our life together.